William Von Bergen

The Rare Coins of America, England, Ireland, Scotland, France, Germany, and Spain

Also, Greek and Roman coins. Sixth Edition

William Von Bergen

The Rare Coins of America, England, Ireland, Scotland, France, Germany, and Spain
Also, Greek and Roman coins. Sixth Edition

ISBN/EAN: 9783337240868

Printed in Europe, USA, Canada, Australia, Japan

Cover: Foto ©Suzi / pixelio.de

More available books at **www.hansebooks.com**

———THE———

RARE COINS OF AMERICA,

ENGLAND, IRELAND, SCOTLAND, FRANCE,

GERMANY, AND SPAIN.

ALSO, GREEK AND ROMAN COINS.

THIS BOOK CONTAINS

A Complete List of, and Prices paid for, Rare American Gold, Silver, Nickel, Brass, Tin and Copper Coins, Fractional Currency, Colonial, Continental and Confederate Paper Money; a List of all Counterfeit U. S. Treasury and National Bank Notes and Canadian Bank Notes, and how to detect them; the Market Value of all Nations' Coins and Bank Notes in U.S. Money; a List and Prices of Rare English, Irish, Scotch, French, German and Spanish Coins. The report of the Coinage of the U. S. Mint for each Fiscal Year from 1793 to 1882.

ILLUSTRATED WITH ABOUT 400 CUTS,

SHOWING OBVERSE AND REVERSE OF EACH GROUP OF RARE COINS, MADE FROM COINS COSTING OVER $6,000.

COPYRIGHT, 1889, BY WM. VON BERGEN.

SIXTH EDITION.

This Edition annuls **all previous ones.** *The prices have been revised according* **to the latest auction sales up to** *June 1, 1891.*

This book contains all information about the Rare Coin Business. Especial attention is called to the explanations in the front part of this book; read and study all carefully, and you will find everything fully explained.

Published by
W. E. SKINNER,
Boston, Mass.

W. E. SKINNER, BOSTON, MASS.

IMPORTANT PREFACE.

Usually the preface of a book is an unnecessary prefix, but this preface is of importance to all who intend to collect coins, currency, etc., for numismatic purposes to sell to dealers in such articles.

The prices quoted beside the dates and descriptions in this book are the current market numismatic values at the date of publishing this book. The publisher of this book, W. E. Skinner, Coin Broker, 325 Washington Street, will usually buy specimens listed herein, and will pay the prices named if he needs the specimens. Almost any other dealer will buy at these rates. It must be remembered that prices are constantly fluctuating. In order to learn the very latest quotations, it is advisable to send ten cents at least once a year to W. E. Skinner for his Premium Coin Manual, which is strictly reliable. This Manual is issued once a year, and is the most reliable publication of its kind.

In sending consignments to a dealer, each piece should be in a separate envelope, labelled, and the lot sent by express or registered mail, with the sender's name and address both inside and on wrapper of package or box.

Dealers are not responsible for consignments if not sent in a safe manner, and if address of sender is not on outside. Moreover, a list of contents should be enclosed and a letter of advice sent by mail at same time in a separate evelope.

W. E. Skinner settles for coins monthly by cheque, draft, money order, stamps or cash in registered letter. Business may be transacted at his office either personally or by mail or express. Distance makes no difference, as his patrons are to be met with in every part of the world. He has clerks competent to conduct correspondence in all ordinary foreign languages.

It is not the date of a coin upon which its value depends so much as its condition. The aim of the numismatist is to get specimens in uncirculated condition whenever possible.

List of other numismatic publications, etc., for sale by W. E. Skinner, Boston: Latest Coin Manual, 10 cents; coin lists, for distribution, containing lists of numerous coins, with prices which you can profitably pay (considerably lower than those quoted in this Gilt Edge Coin Book or manual), 5 cents per dozen, or 25 cents per hundred; Small Foreign Coin Guide, 10 cents; Alexander's Coin Book, 10 cents; Morey's Coin Buying and Selling List, 10 cents; Coin Collector's Herald, 10 cents.

In order to become expert at determining the conditions of coins, it will be advisable to get a sample set, which contains specimens of *uncirculated* and *good* coins, also accurate descriptions of *proofs* and other directions. With the samples and directions much time and expense may be saved. A Sample Coin Set may be bought of W. E. Skinner, Boston. Price per set, 25 cents, postpaid.

Gilt Edge Coin Book. This book can be readily sold by agents. The regular price is two dollars, but some agents sell at a dollar a copy, just half price, and yet earn a good profit. Our price to agents and dealers, at wholesale, is $7.20 per dozen, or in large lots at $50 per 100. No less than 50 sold at the hundred rate. Address all orders to W. E. Skinner, Boston.

Do not write to dealers asking questions about numismatic specimens unless you are sure that the subject is not fully answered in this book. If you find it necessary to write, however, be sure to enclose two 2-cent stamps for reply.

RARE COINS.

The prices paid for rare coins are regulated by their state of preservation and the number of a certain issue in existence; neither the metal out of which the coin is made, nor the age, has anything to do with the prices paid; thus a copper coin might be worth a hundred times more than a gold coin of the same date. A coin issued only a few years ago is often worth more than one 2000 years old. Uncirculated coins of certain dates are worth from $5 to $100, while others of exactly the same kind, but much worn, would not be worth more than their face value.

Rare coins are divided in classes according to their state of preservation, the highest possible state a coin can be in is *proof*, then come *uncirculated*, *fine*, *good*, *fair* and *poor*.

PROOF COINS.

These coins are especially struck for coin collectors. The planchet and dies are polished before the coin is struck, which gives them a burnished or mirror-like, reflective surface. The Mint makes a small charge for each coin so struck, and they can only be had during the year of the issue.

UNCIRCULATED COINS

are coins as they came from the Mint. They must have the same luster as when dropped from the coining press. A coin that has been tarnished and polished up again can not be classed as uncirculated, although it does not show the slightest wear.

FINE COINS

are those that have lost their original luster, but do not show the least wear. They might be tarnished or blackened, but no scratches or nicks are permissible on a fine coin.

GOOD COINS

must show every feature, especially the date, very plain, not scratched, hammered, plugged or otherwise mutilated.

FAIR COINS

are coins on which the lettering, design and date are clearly readable.

POOR COINS

are those on which the design, lettering and date are almost unintelligible.

MUTILATED COINS

are coins with holes, cuts, scratches, hammered or otherwise damaged, and, unless they are coins of a very rare issue, are only worth their intrinsic value. A rare coin with a hole is worth about one-half of what it would be without it.

FOREIGN COINS.

There are very few of the modern foreign coins that command a premium, but any coin issued before 1600 will be bought at a premium. To give a list of all the foreign coins would require a book of several thousand pages, and would be of little value to American collectors.

TO PARTIES FORMING COLLECTIONS OF COINS.

The large shipments of coins I am constantly receiving enables me to fill orders promptly. I have at all times a large stock of the early Colonial copper and silver coins. United States gold, silver and copper coins, ancient Greek, Roman and Mediæval coins, Colonial and Confederate bills, fractional currency and numismatic books.

NEVER CLEAN A COIN IF YOU WANT TO SELL IT TO ME.

COUNTERFEIT RARE COINS.

False coins may be divided into the following classes:

I. RE-STRIKES

are coins made with the original dies, but at a later period. Among the American coins we find re-strikes of the early Colonials, the dollars of 1804, and the half cents of 1831, 1836, 1840 to 1849. They do not command the same price as those struck at the time of the date. At present the dies are destroyed after each year, also all the old dies were destroyed some twenty years ago, and collectors having rare dates can feel safe that there will be no more re-strikes.

II. FORGERIES STRUCK FROM FALSE DIES.

Those are found mostly among the New England shillings, New England sixpence, New England threepence, Pine and Oak Tree Massachusetts coins, Good Samaritan shilling, Sommers Island coins, Carolina Elephant coins, and cent of 1804. No expert in coins is apt to be deceived by them, as their appearance is entirely different from the genuine. They do not have the ancient characteristic peculiarities; the lettering and design is a good deal sharper than on the genuine and the weight is also mostly incorrect.

III. CASTS MADE FROM ORIGINALS.

A cast coin, when in gold or silver, may always be detected by its light weight, unless this has been compensated for by making the cast thicker than the original. The lettering and the types on cast coins are also less sharply defined than on struck coins, and the surface has either a soft and soapy appearance, or else is covered with minute sand holes—an infallible indication of rough casting.

IV. ELECTROTYPES.

These are of necessity of wrong weight. They may also be known by the edges, where the mark of joining of the two sides, separately made and then stuck together, is never concealed, unless, which is seldom the case, the electrotype is intended to deceive. The genuine patina on bronze coins is imitated by paint, which can be removed by spirits of wine. Electrotypes may generally be split in two with a strong knife.

V. ALTERED DATES.

Original coins which have been tooled or altered may be claimed as forgeries. Among the American coins it is especially the dollars of 1801 which are altered by removing the 1 and inserting in its place a 4, and so producing an 1804 dollar. Alterations also occur on the 1793, 1799, 1804 cents, quarter dollars of 1823, 1827 and 1853. These alterations can generally each be detected with a strong magnifying glass, as it hardly ever can be done without leaving some scratches or marks, and anyone buying a rare coin will do well to examine particularly the date.

NO RESPONSIBLE COIN DEALER

will knowingly sell a false coin as genuine, but it nas occurred that coins pronounced genuine by the most experienced turned out to be false, and if ever any case like this should occur in my business, I shall always be ready to take back the coin and refund the money paid for it.

HOW TO SEND COINS.

In order not to go to useless expense, always send a list, and if convenient a rubbing of what you have before sending the coins, and if there is anything among them that I want, I will inform you by return mail.

SMALL LOTS OF COINS

up to one pound in weight are best sent by mail, at one cent per ounce, and if the coins are valuable it is best to have the package registered.

Put up all packages in strong manilla envelopes or in wood or tin boxes. Never send coins in the common white envelopes, as they are not strong enough to hold the coins. I am receiving constantly mail packages broken and some of the coins lost, and I will not be responsible for any loss occurring that way.

LARGE PACKAGES MIGHT BE SENT BY EXPRESS PREPAID.

I positively do not accept packages on which the charges are not paid by the sender, as it often occurs that a person sends a lot of foreign copper coins which are not worth the express charges. *Neither do I accept any packages sent C. O. D.*

All coins are paid for the same day as received and coins once paid for can not be reclaimed.

Anyone that is not satisfied with these terms I do not solicit their business.

Always send your full *name and address* with each lot of coins you send and state the lowest price you will accept for them.

COMMON COINS,

that is, coins which do not command a premium, are returned at the expense of the sender, deducting enough from the amount sent to pay return postage, or I will send check for face value.

THE AMERICAN COIN SCALE.

Coins are generally measured by the above scale; thus a half dollar of the present issue would be called *size* 20, a quarter, *size* 15.

TERMS USED TO DEFINE THE VARIOUS PARTS OF A COIN.

The front or face of a coin is called the *obverse*. O. Obv.

The back is called the *reverse*. R. Rev.

The principal device or object represented on a coin is called the *type*.

The area or space between the type and the circumference is called the *field*.

The lower portion of the area of a coin beneath the type and separated from the rest of the field by a horizontal line is called the *exergue*. *Ex.* This particular place on coins, with or without the separating line, is commonly referred to as the *Ex*.

Small objects represented either in the field or the exergue as adjuncts to the main type are called *symbols*.

Portions of a coin which are sunk below the level of the surface are said to be *incuse*.

THE PRICES QUOTED

in this book include in every instance the face value of the coin, and the publisher reserves the right to change the prices paid at any time without further notice.

The First Metallic Coins

made in America were the New England shilling, sixpence and threepence. They consist of planchets of silver having N. E. stamped on one side and XII., VI., or III. on the other. They were authorized by the General Court of Massachusetts, at Boston, May 27, 1652 On June 20, 1652, an order was issued for the construction of a house for the "Mint," which eventually was built just south of the entrance to the present Pembroke Square, on land belonging to John Hull. The building, when completed, measured sixteen feet square and ten feet high. On June 11, John Hull and Robert Sandersons were sworn in as officers of the Mint, and they were to receive one shilling and sixpence for every twenty shillings coined. The shillings were to weigh seventy-two grains, fineness nine hundred and twenty-five, and the sixpence and threepence in proportion. There is no date on these coins, but they were coined the same year as authorized, and only a limited number were issued of the above type, and the dies changed the same year to the Willow, Oak and Pine Tree coins, which all bear the date of 1652 or 1662, but had been coined for nearly thirty years.

	Uncirculated.	Fine.	Good.
N. E. XII	$30 00	$15 00	$ 5 00
N. E. VI	50 00	25 00	10 00
N. E. III	75 00	30 00	15 00

There are numerous counterfeits of these coins, but they can easily be distinguished by their symmetrical appearance. The originals are clipped into an irregular, round shape and the N. E. and numerals are never opposite each other, but at the side, or one on top and the other at the bottom.

Massachusetts Pine, Oak and Willow Tree Coins.

	Uncirculated.	Fine.	Good.
MASSACHUSETTS: Willow-tree Shilling: large centre-mark in tree: roots oblique to right: MASATHVSETS. IN. R 1652 | XII in circle of connected pellets: NEW ENGLAND AN DOM.: letters and figures broad,	$25 00	$10 00	$5 00

                                    Uncirculated. Fine.   Good.
Willow-tree Shilling: roots of tree
  point downward: MASA HVETS
  IN. ℞ date in thin figures:
  NEW LIN AND . NDO: broad plan-
  chet $15 00 $5 00 $3 00
Willow-tree Sixpence: similar
  type: MMASATVSETSS IN 15 00   5 00   3 00
Willow-tree Threepence: bushy
  tree formed of curves and with
  the characteristic central dot
  which marks the preceding
  coins of this type: MASAT VSETS
  · IN. ℞ 165(2) | III in circle of
  ined pellets: NEW ENGLAND, 25 00   15 00   5 00

Oak-tree Shilling: roots point
  downward: top branch points
  between H V. ℞ large "6" in
  date....................... $5 00 $3 00 $2 00
Oak-tree Shilling: 3 forked roots
  l.: top branch points at right
  foot of H. ℞ same as next pre-
  ceding..................... 5 00   3 00   2 00
Oak-tree Shilling: crossed roots:
  top branch forked: very large
  letters. ℞ same as last....... 6 00   3 00   2 00
Oak-tree Shilling: crossed roots:
  top branch below H: one sprout
  or sucker left of tree. ℞ small
  thick "I" in date: AN smaller
  than other letters............ 5 00   3 00   2 00
Oak-tree Shilling: roots crossed:
  sucker each side of tree. ℞
  widely spaced thin figures in
  date: 6 has extra outlines:
  small letters. 8 00   5 00   3 00

	Uncirculated.	Fine.	Good.
Oak-tree Shilling : 5 roots l. : fewer branches to tree. ℞ broad, irregular lettering : no centre-mark	$5 00	$3 00	$2 00
Oak-tree Shilling : roots r. : numerous branches to tree : topmost points to MA. ℞ GL below the value.	5 00	3 00	2 00
Oak-tree Shilling : same obv. as last. ℞ ND below value : pellets in circle connected.	6 00	4 00	2 00
Oak-tree Sixpence : highest branch points to left foot of H : first s reversed. ℞ 652 of date large : the 1 small : No below,	15 00	8 00	4 00
Oak-tree Sixpence : no suckers beside tree. ℞ date near top of circle, 2 resembles O.	10 00	5 00	3 00

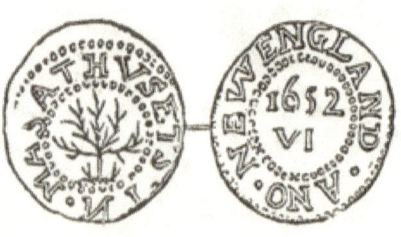

Oak-tree Sixpence : two roots and sucker each side of tree in oval of connected pellets : topmost branch points between TH. ℞ date and value well centred : LA below : broad planchet.	$10 00	$5 00	$3 00
Oak-tree Threepence : peculiar willowy tree : all S's reversed. ℞ large date and letters.	6 00	3 00	2 00
Oak-tree Threepence : rudely formed tree : first s reversed. ℞ thin figures in date : 2 small,	8 00	4 00	3 00
Oak-tree Threepence : well-formed tree : sucker r. : 5 roots l. ℞ 36 pellets in circle.	7 00	3 00	2 00

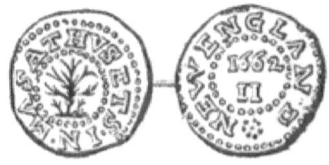

	Uncirculated.	Fine.	Good
Oak-tree Twopence..............	$5 00	$3 00	$3 00
Oak-tree Twopence: differs slightly from last: date smaller.....	5 00	3 00	2 00

Pine-tree Shilling, 1650: pine-tree with cones on branches: MASSACHVSETS * IN * . ℞ 1650 | — | XII in circle of large oval pellets: NEW ENGLAND * AN. DO *	$10 00	$5 00	$3 00
Pine-tree Shilling, 1650: small tree in circle of connected pellets: MASATHVSETS+IN+. ℞ 1650 | XII in similar circle: NEW ENGLAND: ANDO: smaller planchet than the preceding..	9 00	4 00	3 00
Pine-tree Shilling: broad planchet: split tree: roots horizontal: top branch below right foot of H. ℞ date and value large and close together: period after each word.............	5 00	3 00	2 00

Pine-tree Shilling: broad: tree split nearly to top: s above: legend MASATVSETS. (*sic*) IM.

	Uncirculated.	Fine.	Good.

℞ small letters and date: all N's reversed: colon after each word. $6 00 $4 00 $2 00

Pine-tree Shilling: broad: large, finely spread tree nearly filling the circle: top branch points left of v: large, clearly cut letters. ℞ OM. below value..... 10 00 5 00 3 00

Pine-tree Shilling: broad: tree narrow and symmetrical: v above roots natural form. ℞ same as that of next preceding........ $8 00 $4 00 $4 00

Pine-tree Shilling: broad: oval tree: 7 roots r. and l.: top branch below right foot of H. ℞ date small, value large: first N in ENGLAND reversed....... 10 00 5 00 3 00

Pine-tree Shilling: peculiarly formed branches on tree: curved-like bows: roots forked. ℞ large date and value................ 15 00 8 00 5 00

Pine-tree Shilling: broad: well-modeled tree in circle of oblong square grains (styled the "Cogwheel"): roots small, well distributed: top below N. ℞ still larger grains to the circle: letters large and crude.......... 25 00 10 00 5 00

Pine-tree shilling: small planchet: smaller oblong square grains than on last, but lettering more crude. 8 00 4 00 2 00

Pine-tree Shilling: broad: tree small, a pellet each side of

	Uncirculated.	Fine.	Good.
trunk: four large roots r.: top branch below s: groups of 7 pellets after IN. ℞ date and letters small................	$10 00	$5 00	$3 00
Pine-tree Shilling in *copper* struck over Geo. I. Halfpenny, 1724: tree with 4 roots l.: heavy leaves on ends of branches: oblong square grains in circle. ℞ large date: small letters in NEW ENGLAD (*sic*) AN. DO.	5 00	3 00	1 00

Pine-tree Shilling: small planchet: wide tree: roots l. small letters: top branch points to right of v. ℞ small date, XII large: AN.D below............	$10 00	$5 00	$2 00
Pine-tree Shilling: small: smaller tree: 5 roots downward: top branch below s: large letters. ℞ from same die as last.......	11 00	6 00	2 00
Pine-tree Shilling: small: broad tree: roots r. and l., two separated: top branch just left of v: large letters. ℞ from same die as last two..................	12 00	6 00	2 00
Pine-tree Sixpence: usual type: broad planchet...............	10 00	5 00	2 00
Pine-tree Sixpence: same dies as last, but smaller planchet.....	8 00	5 00	2 00
Pine-tree Sixpence: broad tree with thorn-like leaves: 4 roots r.: top branch below s. ℞ from same die as that used for rev. of Oaktree........................	25 00	10 00	5 00
Pine-tree Threepence: pellet each			

	Uncirculated.	Fine.	Good.
side of tree: large wide letters. ℞ group of 4 pellets after D....	$10 00	$5 00	$2 00
Pine-tree Threepence: no pellets beside tree: 4 roots l.: thin letters. ℞ group of 7 pellets after D......................	10 00	5 00	2 00
Pine-tree Threepence: large tree in circle, separating the value III. | PENCE: in outer circle: PROVINCE OF THE ' MASSACHUSETTS. ℞ same design, from same die....................	3 00	2 00	1 00

Good Samaritan Shilling: view of the Samaritan anointing the wounds of a man under a tree: MASATHVSETS .... IN. ℞ 1652 | XII in circle of connected pellets: IN NEW ENGLAND ANO:	$100 00	$50 00	$25 00

Maryland Coins.

Issued under Cecil the Second, Lord Baltimore. They have no date, but are supposed to have been coined in 1659.

	Uncirculated.	Fine.	Good.
MARYLAND: Shilling: draped bust of Lord Baltimore l. ✠			

	Uncirculated.	Fine.	Good.
CÆCILIVS : DNS : TERRÆMARIÆ : &CT. ℞ crown shield of arms separating XII : CRESCITE : ET : MVLTIPLICAMINI	$30 00	$15 00	$3 00
Sixpence : similar type : value VI : no period after MULTIPLICAMINI : lacks the T in &CT	20 00	10 00	2 00
Sixpence : similar type, but legend reads MVLTILICAMINI.(sic), the P being omitted	40 00	25 00	5 00
Groat : similar type : value IV	50 00	25 00	5 00

Penny : obv. similar to that of the sixpence. ℞ two pennants upon a coronet : DENARIVM : TERRÆ-MARIÆ ✠ : copper $100 00 $50 00 $25 00

Shilling : radiant eye over liberty-cap on pole between two stars and surrounded by 13 interlinked rings with 11 stars. ℞ in script, *Equal,(to | one) Shi:* clasped hands below : I. CHALMERS * ANNAPOLIS * 1783 * . $50 00 $25 00 $10 00

	Uncirculated.	Fine.	Good.
Shilling: two birds with long worm on river-bank: ONE * SHILLING: 1783. ℞ clasped hands in wreath: I. CHALMERS, ANNAPOLIS *	$10 00	3 00	1 00
Shilling· similar type, but larger birds, shorter worm	6 00	2 00	1 00

Sixpence: star in wreath: I. CHALMERS. ANNAPOLIS. ℞ cross with floreated angles, stars and crescents on terminations: T S in the crescents: I. C. | SIX | PENCE | 1783 (small date): divided by arms of the cross	$15 00	$5 00	$2 00
Sixpence: similar type, but larger date: different die	10 00	3 00	1 00

Threepence: clasped hands: I. CHALMERS. ANNAP'S *. ℞ branch in wreath: three * pence · 1783	$5 00	$2 00	$1 00

                                      Uncirculated. Fine. Good.

Threepence: draped bust l.: BALTIMORE ˙ TOWN ˙ JULY ˙ 4 ˙ 90. ℞ THREE | PENCE in circle: STANDISH BARRY: letters interlaced with beadwork $25 00 $10 00 $5 00

Colonial and Continental Copper Coins.

Sommer Islands Shilling.

First coin made for America, in memory of Sir George Sommers, who was shipwrecked upon the Bermudas or Sommer Islands in 1612. They are made of brass—shilling, sixpence and threepence. They bear no date, but are supposed to have been coined 1616.

	Uncirculated.	Fine.	Good.
SOMMER ISLANDS: Shilling: ship sailing. ℞ wild boar l: XII. above: SOMMER * ISLANDS : thick planchet: copper: size 20	$100 00	$50 00	$20 00
Shilling: larger ship. ℞ same as last: thin planchet: copper: size 20	80 00	30 00	15 00
Sixpence: similar type: VI over boar: ILANDS (*sic*). ℞ heraldic flowers below ship: copper: size 17	70 00	25 00	15 00
Threepence: similar type, but without legend: III over boar,	70 00	25 00	15 00

Carolina Elephant Copper.

	Uncirculated.	Fine.	Good.
CAROLINA: Halfpenny, 1694: elephant l. ℞ GOD: | PRESERVE: | CAROLINA: AND | THE LORDS: | PROPRIETERS. | 1694 : size 16	$100 00	$50 00	$20 00
Halfpenny, 1694: same as preceding, except that "E" in proprieters was altered in the die: it now reads PROPRIETORS : size 19	50 00	25 00	10 00
NEW ENGLAND: Halfpenny: elephant l. ℞ GOD: | PRESERVE: | (new) | ENGLAND: | 1694;	100 00	50 00	20 00
LONDON: Halfpenny token: elephant l., same die as Carolina ½d. 1694. ℞ city arms on shield: LONDON: GOD: PRESERVE: *: very thick planchet,	3 00	2 00	50

French Colonial Coins of Louis XV.

	Uncirculated.	Fine.	Good.
LOUISIANA: Sou, 1721: crossed L's crowned. ℞ date between two ornaments: *mint-mark* B (Rouen)	$2 00	$1 00	25
Sou 1721: type of preceding, minus ornaments at date: *m. m.* H (Rochelle)	2 00	1 00	25

Sou, 1767: without R. F.	$5 00	$3 00	$1 00
Sou, 1767: with R. F.	1 00	50	25
¼ Dollar: heraldic eagle: NOUVELLE ORLEANS. R P. B. in circle of 16 stars and links: counterstamped on section of Spanish dollar:	10 00	5 00	2 00
¼ Dollar: similar designs but different counterstamps: with additional stamp "*Bad*"	4 00	2 00	1 00

Rosa Americana Money.

Made by William Wood.

	Uncirculated.	Fine.	Good.
Twopence, 1717: laureated bust of Geo. I. r. in armor: GEORGIVS. D : G M : B : FR : ET . II : REX. ℞ large II beneath crown in circle: legend in outer circle, 1717: MAG . BRIT . FRA . ET . HIDER . REX : yellow bronze	$15 00	$8 00	$3 00
Penny (n. d.): laur. nude bust George I. r.: GEORGIVS . D : G : M : BRI . FRA : ET . HIB : REX. ℞ large I below crown : DAT . PACEM . ET . NOUAS . PREBET . ET . AUGET . OPES. : bronze	15 00	8 00	3 00
Penny (n. d.): obv. from same die as last. ℞ large I between laurel branches, crown above: BRVN : ET . LVN : DVX . SA : ROM : MI : ARC═THE : ET . PR : ELEC . : bronze	10 00	5 00	2 00
Halfpenny: (n. d.) small bust of George I. r.: laureated and mailed : GEORGIVS . REX. ℞ ½ beneath crown : . DAT . PACEM . ET . AUGET . OPES. : bronze	15 00	8 00	3 00

Twopence (n. d.): large nude bust of Geo. I. r. : laureated : GEORGIUS . DEI . GRATIA REX. ℞ a rose-bush, with one full and

	Uncirculated.	Fine.	Good.
two half-blown roses and three buds: ROSA: SINE: SPINA.: bronze....................	$50 00	$30 00	$15 00
Twopence (n. d.) : large nude bust of Geo. I. r. : laureated : GEORGIVS . D: G: MAG: BRI: FRA: ET . HIB: REX. ℞ heraldic rose: . ROSA . AMERICANA. |. UTILE . DULCI (in field) struck without a die collar, on a very broad planchet : size 24 : copper,	25 00	15 00	5 00
Twopence (n. d.) : same legend no period after REX: entirely different portrait. ℞ from same die as that next preceding : bronze: size 20..............	25 00	15 00	5 00
Twopence (n. d.) : obv. very similar to last : period after REX. ℞ smaller rose : UTILE . DULCI *on label* below, smaller letters and without the periods before and after : bronze	5 00	2 00	1 00
Twopence, 1722 : similar obv., but from different die. ℞ similar to last, with date added and legend differently placed : yellow bronze...................	5 00	2 00	1 00
Penny, 1722 : similar bust, but smaller : GEORGIVS . DEI . GRATIA . REX. : E under lowest curl. ℞ heraldic rose : ROSA . AMERICANA * VTILE . DVLCI .: 1722 * : yellow bronze..............	10 00	5 00	2 00
Penny, 1722 : same type as last : different obv. die : G under lowest curl : yellow bronze.......	4 00	2 00	50
Penny, 1722 : similar type : point of bust rounded. ℞ smaller letters : period before UTILE DULCI. : wide planchet with *obliquely milled edge:* bronze : size 17½.....................	15 00	8 00	3 00
Penny, 1722 : similar type, differing die : pointed bust : plain edges : bronze : size 17........	2 00	1 00	50

	Uncirculated.	Fine.	Good.
Penny, 1722: similar type: * before UTILE . DULCI.: bronze...	$3 00	$2 00	$0 50
Halfpenny, 1722: smaller bust r. GEORGIUS . DEI . GRATIA . REX. ℞ heraldic rose : ROSA . AMERI . VTILE . DVLCI . 1722: bronze,	10 00	5 00	2 00
Halfpenny, 1722: similar profile: GEORGIUS . D : G : REX. ℞ heraldic rose : ROSA . AMERI : UTILE . DULCI . 1722................	8 00	3 00	1 00
Halfpenny, 1722: similar to obv. but larger letters. ℞ heraldic rose : ROSA . AMERICANA . UTILE . DULCI . 1722 * : yellow bronze,	3 00	1 00	50
Twopence, 1723: crowned rose: cross beneath I : size 21.......	5 00	2 00	50
Twopence, 1723: same as last, but planchet not so broad : size 20.	5 00	2 00	50
Twopence, 1723: same type : cross beneath RI.	5 00	2 00	50
Twopence, 1723: same type: X. distant from bust............	8 00	3 00	1 00
Twopence, 1723: same type: no period after REX, the X touches bust : yellow bronze..........	8 00	3 00	1 00
Halfpenny, 1723: same type: crowned rose : UTILE . DULCI on ribbon : *silver*...............	25 00	10 00	5 00
Halfpenny, 1723: same type, but different dies : copper........	1 00	50	25
Halfpenny, 1723: similar obv. ℞ *uncrowned* rose UTILE DULCI in field : 1723 over 1722.......	10 00	5 00	1 00
Halfpenny, 1723: same type as last : *uncrowned* rose : obv. die slightly different. ℞ same as last.........................	2 00	1 00	50
Penny, 1724: similar to crowned rose type of preceding year : G close below lowest curl : period after REX. ℞ colon after ROSA : large cross on crown divides AME RICANA : 1724 over 1723 : in *silver*.....................	40 00	20 00	10 00
Penny, 1724: similar type, but portrait differently engraved :			

	Uncirculated.	Fine.	Good.

G to left of lowest curl: no period after REX, the x touches the bust. ℞ from same die as last: bronze.................... $20 00 $10 00 $5 00

Twopence, 1733: laureated nude bust of Geo. II. l.: GEORGIVS . II . D . G . REX. ℞ full-blown rose on branch, bud r.: crown above: UTILE DULCI. on ribbon below: ROSA . AMERICANA . 1733...................... $100 00 $50 00 $25 00

WOOD'S IRISH SERIES.

(Refused in Ireland and sent to America.)

These undoubtedly passed for Pence and Halfpence, although intended originally for Halfpence and Farthings—by these latter names we quote them.

Uncirculated. Fine. Good.

Halfpenny, 1722: laureated profile r.: long neck, nude bust: GEORGIVS D: G: REX. in large letters. ℞ Hibernia seated with harp on *left*, looks toward pile of rocks on right: . HIBERNIÆ . : date in ex................. $20 00 $10 00 $5 00

	Uncirculated.	Fine.	Good.
Halfpenny, 1722, different profile. shorter neck: smaller letters: GEORGIUS . DEI. GRATIA . REX. ℞ Hibernia seated facing her . harp on left: legend above: HIBERNIA . 1722	$5 00	$3 00	$1 00

Halfpenny, 1722: similar obv. ℞ Hibernia seated l. holds palm branch, and rests on harp at right: legend beginning near feet on left...................	3 00	2 00	1 00
Halfpennies, 1723, same type as last: large and small planchets,	1 00	50	10
Farthing, 1723: same type: struck in *silver*....................	15 00	10 00	5 00
Farthing, 1723: same type: copper.........................	10 00	5 00	1 00
Halfpenny, 1724: same type: struck in *silver*..............	15 00	10 00	5 00
Halfpenny, 1724: same type: period after date: copper.....	1 00	50	10
Farthings, 1724: same type......	1 00	50	10

Mark Newby New Jersey Coins.

Brought from Ireland in 1682.

	Uncirculated.	Fine.	Good.
NEW JERSEY: Mark Newby Shilling: royal harpist kneeling before a crown: FLOREAT: REX. ℞ St. Patrick, with double cross: drives reptiles before him: church r.: QVIESCAT PLEBS: *silver*	$15 00	$8 00	$3 00
Mark Newby Shilling: similar type but letters larger: I touches top of the mitre: *silver*: planchet broader	10 00	5 00	2 00
Mark Newby Halfpenny: type of preceding: bronze	2 00	1 00	25
Mark Newby Halfpenny: large royal harpist. ℞ St. Patrick with crook and shamrock before the people: Dublin arms on shield r. ECCE GREX	2 00	1 00	25
Cent, 1786: female seated on globe r. holds flag and balance: IMMUNIS COLUMBIA. ℞ broad shield: * E * PLURIBUS * UNUM *	50 00	25 00	10 00
Cent: draped bust of Washington r.: GEN. WASHINGTON. ℞ same as that of last	150 00	80 00	50 00
Cent: smaller bust of Washington r. (non) VI VIRTUTE VICI.: differing considerably from the N. Y. design of this type, the head being much wider. ℞ medium small shield	50 00	25 00	10 00

	Uncirculated.	Fine.	Good
Cent, 1786: small bust of horse r. close to very heavy plow: no punctuation: date in very small figures *under the beam*, and sloping toward lower edge. ℞ broad shield: left corner opposite foot of R.............	$150 00	$80 00	$50 00
Cent, 1786: still smaller bust of horse r., more distant from plow: the single-tree horizontal: *date under beam* in larger figures, curving upward: period after CÆSAREA. ℞ similar to that of last, but shield more rounded: left corner opposite tail of R.............	200 00	100 00	50 00

1786 Cent: bust of horse r. over plow, curved beam, ℞ shield..	$1 00	50	10
1786, bust of horse r. over plow: curved beam, no coulter......	1 00	50	10
1786, bust of horse r. over plow: straight beam................	1 00	50	10
1787, bust of horse r. over plow: straight beam................	1 00	50	10
1787, bust of horse r. over plow: curved beam.................	1 00	50	10
1787, bust of horse r. over plow: curved beam: single tree points l. downward.................	2 00	1 00	50
1787, bust of horse r. over plow: curved beam, with sprig.....	1 00	50	10

	Uncirculated.	Fine.	Good.
1787, bust horse r. over plow: curved beam: sprig: PLURIBS,	$2 00	$1 00	$ 50
1788, bust horse r. over plow: straight beam	1 00	50	10
1788, bust horse r. over plow: straight beam. R has minute fox on l.	2 00	1 00	50
1788, bust horse r. over plow: straight beam. R has minute fox on r.	10 00	5 00	2 00
1788, bust horse r. over plow: curved beam	1 00	50	10
1788, bust horse l. over plow, curved beam	$2 00	$1 00	$0 50

Connecticut Deer and Hammer Coins.

Made by John Higley, at Granby, Connect'cut, from 1737 to 1739, and thought to be the first copper coins made in America. All are extremely rare.

	Uncirculated.	Fine.	Good.
CONNECTICUT: Threepence, 1737: deer standing l. in circle: ☛ THE . VALVE . OF . THREE . PENCE. R three crowned hammers in circle: * CONNECTICVT . 1737	$100 00	$50 00	$15 00
Threepence, 1737: same obv. as last. R three crowned hammers: ☛ I . AM . (good) COPPER . 1737	80 00	30 00	10 00
Threepence, 1737: deer standing l. club-like flaw in die in field: ☛ VALVE . ME . AS . YOU .			

	Uncirculated.	Fine.	Good.

PLEASE . * III . ℞ three crowned hammers: 👉 . 1 . AM . GOOD . COPPER . * 1737, $50 00 $20 00 $10 00

Threepence: deer standing l.:
VALUE . ME . (as y) OU . PLEASE
. * III. ℞ broad-axe: J . CUT
(my) WAY . THRO (ugh) 1739, $50 00 $20 00 $10 00
Threepence: same obv. as last:
(va)LUE . ME . AS . YOU (plea)
SE * III. ℞ broad-axe barely
touches circle: 👉 (J. C)UT .
MY . WAY . THROUGH 50 00 20 00 10 00

Connecticut State Cent.

Coined from 1785 to 1788 inclusive; each year varies somewhat in design. They all have: Bust, Auctori Connect.

	Uncirculated.	Fine.	Good.
1785 Cent: mailed bust l. ℞, female seated l. (on all)	$0 75	$0 25	$0 10
1785, mailed bust r. small date...	50	15	5
1785, mailed bust r. large date...	25	10	5

	Uncirculated.	Fine.	Good.
1786, mailed bust r.	$0 25	$0 10	$0 5
1786, mailed bust r. ℞ ET LIB INDE	50	25	10
1786, mailed bust l.	25	10	5
1786, draped bust l.	30	15	10
1787, mailed bust r.	25	10	5
1787, mailed bust r. ℞ ET LIB INDE	25	10	5
1787, mailed bust l.	25	10	5
1787, mailed bust l. ℞ INDE	25	10	5
1787, mailed bust l. CONNECT	50	25	10
1787, mailed bust l. CONNECT. ℞ IND	50	25	10
1787, mailed bust l. CONNECT. ℞ INDL	50	25	10
1787, draped bust l. large letters	25	10	5
1787, draped bust l. small letters	25	10	5
1787, draped bust l. small letters. ℞ LIR	25	10	5
1787, draped bust l. AUCIORI	50	25	10
1787, draped bust l. AUCTOBI	50	25	10
1787, draped bust l. AUCTOBI. ℞ LIR	50	25	10
1787, draped bust l. AUCTOPI	75	50	25
1787, draped bust l. AUCTOPI. ℞ IIB	50	25	10
1787, draped bust l. CONNFC	25	10	05
1787, draped bust l. ℞ FNDE	75	50	25
1788, mailed bust r.	25	10	05
1788, mailed bust l.	25	10	05
1788, mailed bust l. CONNLC	50	25	10
1788, draped bust l. large letters,	25	10	05
1788, draped bust l. small letters,	25	10	05
1788, draped bust l. ℞ INDL,	50	25	10

Virginia Coins.

	Uncirculated.	Fine.	Good.
VIRGINIA: Shilling, 1774: nude bust of Geo. III., laureated, r. ℞ British arms on garnished shield crowned: VIRGI NIA. 17 74: *silver*	$75 00	$50 00	$25 00
Penny, 1773: same type as last, with addition of dentated border.	1 00	25	10

	Uncirculated.	Fine.	Good.

Halfpence, 1773: same types but from differing dies: sizes 16 to 16½................. $1 00 $0 25 $0 10

Shilling: view of Gloucester Court House: XII below: GLOVCESTER . CO. (——) VIRGINIA. ℞ large star ★ RIC DAWSON . ANNO . DOM . 1714.......... 20 00   10 00   5 00

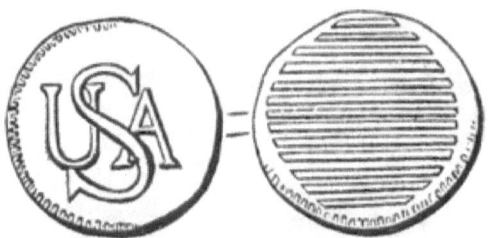

United States Bar Cent.

Made in England in 1785 and sent to New York for circulation.

	Uncirculated.	Fine.	Good.

Monogram U. S. A. 13 bars..... $5 00 $2 00 $0 50

There are numerous counterfeits of this coin.

Vermont Cents.

	Uncirculated.	Fine.	Good.

VERMONT: Cent, 1785: mailed bust r.: AERMON VUCTORI. ℞ Liberty seated r.: IMMUNE COLUMBIA: 1785: in ex....... $5 00 $2 00 $1 00

Cent, 1785: sun rising from *left* of thickly wooded mountain: date in ex., 1785: VERMONTIS RES PUBLICA. ℞ radiant *sun*, pointed rays, with alternate stars: STELLA QUARTA DECIMA, in large letters............. $10 00 $5 00 $2 00

Cent, 1785: sun rising to right behind mountains: 8 trees: plow below: VERMONTS . RES . PUBLICA . 1785. ℞ radiant eye, broad, forked rays: QUARTA . DECIMA . STELLA....... $10 00 $5 00 $2 00
Cent, 1785: same type as last, but "VERMONTIS".............. 10 00 5 00 1 00

	Uncirculated.	Fine.	Good.
Cent, 1785: thicker planchet.....	$5 00	$2 00	$0 50
Cent, 1785: same type, VERMONTIS. ℞ *from same die as the obverse*.......................	3 00	1 00	25

Cent, 1786: sun higher: 7 trees: VERMONTENSIUM. ℞ radiant eye: pointed groups of rays: same legend as on preceding types........................	$5 00	$1 00	$0 25
Cent, 1786: same type, but with 9 trees: P touches tree on right. ℞ similar to that of last, but from different die.............	5 00	1 00	25
Cent, 1786: same type: 9 trees, but from different dies: 1 in date cut twice in die. ℞ same as last.......................	5 00	1 00	25

Cent, 1786: the "Baby-head": infantile bust r.: AUCTORI: VERMON. ℞ rudely executed seated

	Uncirculated.	Fine.	Good.
figure l.: INDE.ET: LIB: 1786,	$3 00	$2 00	$0 50
Cent: the "Baby-head": obv. and rev. struck from same die.....	3 00	2 00	50
Cent, 1786: mailed bust l.: VERMON: AUCTORI: ℞ seated figure l.: INDE ET LIB | 1786....	2 00	1 00	25
Cents, 1786: similar type, but no colon after AUCTORI. ℞ colon after INDE: and LIB..........	1 00	50	25
Cents, 1787: mailed busts r.: no punctuations either side: large and small planchets..........	1 00	50	25
Cents, 1787: similar types: periods after VERMON. AUCTORI. ℞ same as those next preceding.....................	1 00	50	25
Cents, 1787: similar obv.: no punctuations. ℞ BRITANNIA.	1 00	50	25
"Tory Cent," 1787: bust of Geo. III. r.: GEORGIVS III. REX. ℞ female seated l. on globe: INDE ✱· ET LIB ✱..........	2 00	1 00	50
Cent, 1788: regular type: no punctuations	1 00	50	25
Cents, 1788: regular type: periods after VERMON . and AUCTORI......................	1 00	50	25
Cents, 1788: similar types: VERMON + AUCTORI + ℞ INDE+ ET · LIB+..................	1 00	50	25
Cent, 1788: curled hair: VERMON AUCTORI ✱ ℞ INDE ✱ ET LIB ✱	3 00	2 00	50
Cent, 1788: VERMON ✱ ✱ AUCTORI ✱ : ℞ INDE+ET·LIB+: struck over Geo. III. ½d.............	2 00	1 00	25
Cent, 1788: ✱ VERMON ✱ ✱ AUCTORI ✱: ℞ same as that of last,	2 00	1 00	25
Cents, 1788: over Geo. III. Irish ½d., 1782...................	1 00	50	25
Tory Cent, 1788: large bust same as obv. 2: GEORGIVS.III.REX. ℞ INDE + ET . LIB + (Rev. B.)............................	2 00	1 00	25

	Uncirculated.	Fine.	Good.
Tory Cent, 1788: small bust Geo. III. r.: GEORGIVS III. REX. ℞ larger seated figure: INDE ✶ ET ✶LIB ✶....................	$2 00	$1 00	$25

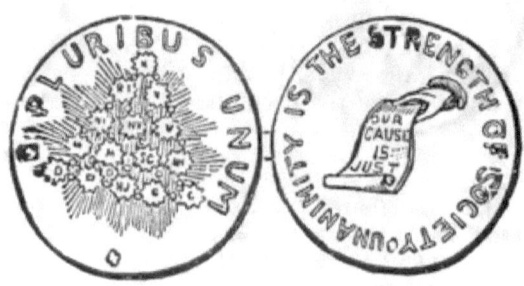

Kentucky Halfpenny.

	Uncirculated.	Fine.	Good.
KENTUCKY: Halfpenny: arm and hand presents scroll inscribed OUR | CAUSE | IS | JUST : legend, UNANIMITY IS THE STRENGTH OF SOCIETY✝. ℞ radiant triangle of 15 stars, each bearing initials of a State: E PLURIBUS UNUM: on edge, PAYABLE IN LANCASTER, LONDON OR BRISTOL..................	$2 00	$1 00	$0 25
Halfpenny: same as next preceding, but edge inscribed, PAYABLE AT BEDWORTH NUNEATON OR (?) KLEY..................	3 00	2 00	1 00
Halfpenny: same type, but edge engrailed, or corded.........	2 00	1 00	25
Halfpenny: same type, but edge plain.......................	2 00	1 00	25

	Proof.	Fine.	Good.
Halfpenny, 1796: forlorn figure of Britannia seated l., her feet upon emblems of Justice: PAYABLE BY P. P. P. MYDDELTON. ℞ Hope presents male and female children to Liberty: BRITISH SETTLEMENT KENTUCKY | 1796: *silver*.................	$20 00	$10 00	$5 00

	Proof.	Fine.	Good.
Halfpenny, 1796: same as last, but in copper	$10 00	$5 00	$1 00

KENTUCKY-CANADA: Halfpenny, 1796: obv. same as reverse of last. ℞ in circle, COPPER | COMPANY | OF UPPER | CANADA: in outer circle ONE HALF PENNY $20 00 $10 00 $5 00

Massachusetts Cent.

	Uncirculated.	Fine.	Good.
MASSACHUSETTS: Cent, 1787: small compact date: arrows on *l.*, olive branch on *r*	$25 00	$10 00	$5 00
Cent, 1787. ℞ 4 leaves on olive branch: 7 arrows on r.: small planchet: size 16	1 00	50	25
Cent, 1787: divided date: 5 leaves on branch: 9 arrows	10 00	5 00	2 00

	Uncirculated.	Fine.	Good.
Cent, 1787: compact date: 13 arrows..................	$6 00	$3 00	$1 00
Half Cent, 1787: 10 arrows: thin figures......................	1 00	50	25
Half Cent, 1787: 12 arrows: broad figures: no period after final s,	1 00	50	25
Cent, 1788: 12 arrows: short 1 in date........................	1 00	50	25
Half Cent, 1788.................	1 00	50	25 .

Cent, 1776: Pine tree. ℞ Liberty seated on globe l..............	$100 00	$50 00	$25 00
NEW ENGLAND: Stiver: two lions on skins : 1 s | v c rev.: New Engla | ND | IM, the N's reversed: M inverted: copper,	10 00	5 00	1 00

New York Brasher Doubloon. Gold.

Uncirculated. Fine. Good.

NEW YORK: Doubloon, 1787: radiant sun over mountain range, sea in foreground: BRASHER in ex.: circle of pellets surrounding: NOVA . EBORACA . COLUMBIA . EXCELSIOR . : quatrefoil after each word. ℞ National arms, heraldic eagle and stars, in laurel wreath: EB in oval counterstamped on left wing UNUM * E * PLURIBUS * 1787 * $500 00 $300 00 $200 00

Doubloon, 1787: same as preceding, except EB on breast of eagle 400 00 300 00 200 00

Penny: spread eagle copied from U. S. Arms: * NEW . YORKE . IN . AMERICA +. ℞ Cupid running toward Psyche: group of 5 palms between: brass. The obverse die was doubtless made

	Uncirculated.	Fine.	Good.

in New York during or shortly after the Revolution, as is indicated by the style of eagle and workmanship: the reverse is of more artistic finish and was no doubt made in France many years before, and intended for the popular jetons then so abundant.................... $5 00 $3 00 $1 00

Cent, 1786: military bust r. of Washington (or Clinton): NON VI VIRTUTI VICI. ℞ Liberty seated r. holds balance and capped pole. NEO-EBORACENSIS. | 1786.................... $50 00 $25 00 $10 00

Cent, 1786: larger head, smaller bust, NON (vi vir) TUTE VICI. ℞ smaller figure of Liberty: (N)EO-EB(ora) CENCIS . | small 1786 in ex............. 50 00   25 00   10 00

Cent, 1787: bust of Gov. Clinton r.: GEORGE * CLINTON * . ℞

	Uncirculated.	Fine.	Good.

State arms on oval shield, surmounted by an eagle r. on section of globe and supported by Liberty and Justice: 1787 | EXCELSIOR in ex................ $100 00 $50 00 $20 00

Cent, 1787: State arms supported by Liberty l. and Justice r.: eagle facing l. on section of globe: EXCELSIOR in ex. ℞ National arms: E. PLURIBUS UNUM * : 1787 between trefoil and star..................... $25 00 $15 00 $5 00

Cent, 1787: same type, but eagle faces *right*................... 25 00 15 00 5 00

Cent, 1787: from same obv. die as that preceding. ℞ National arms larger: stars differently placed: olive branch on r.: arrows l.: date smaller and between stars.................. 25 00 15 00 5 00

Cent, 1787: Indian standing l. holds bow and tomahawk:

	Uncirculated.	Fine.	Good.

LIBER NATUS LIBERTATEM DEFENDO ✶ . ℞ same as on George Clinton cut............$80 00 $50 00 $25 00

Cent, 1787: same obv. ℞ eagle (or crow) with mis-mated wings standing on section of globe: NEO-EBORACUS 1787 | EXCELSIOR...................... 80 00 50 00 25 00

Cent: same obv.: ℞ bust of George III. r.: CEOR (civs) III REX........................ 15 00 5 00 1 00

Cent, 1787: laureated mailed bust r.: ✶ NOVA ✶ EBORACE ✶ . ℞ Liberty seated r. on globe: State arms on shield at her side: ✶ VERT ET . LIB ∴ | 1787...................... $5 00 $1 00 $0 25

Cent, 1787: same obv. ℞ Liberty seated l., with heavier drapery: same legend and date, but differently spaced: period after VIRT........................ 5 00 1 00 25

Cent, 1787: small bust: legend punctuated with stars instead of quatrefoils. ℞ smaller figure of Liberty seated l. ✶ VIRT. ET. LIB ✶ : ET is above the head: date in ex. 1787.... 30 00 15 00 5 00

Cent, 1787: larger bust: *two* quatrefoils before NOVA (none after). ℞ larger figure of Liberty: shield border of scale-armor pattern: period between LIB and the quatrefoil........ 20 00 10 00 3 00

Mott's Token.

	Uncirculated.	Fine.	Good.
Cent, 1789: clock. ℞ Heraldic eagle....................	$1 00	$0 25	$0 10

Talbot, Allum & Lee Token.

	Uncirculated.	Fine.	Good.
Cent, 1794: Liberty standing. ℞ Ship r. : Talbot, Allum & Lee,	$1 00	$0 50	$0 25
Cent, 1794: Liberty standing. ℞ Ship r.: NEW YORK above ship.....................	50	25	10
Cent, 1795: Liberty standing. ℞ Ship r.: NEW YORK below ship	75	30	15

There are several scarce mulings of the two last obverses, with English Halfpence.

Uncirculated. Fine. Good.

NOVA CONSTELLATIO: Dollar, or 1000 Mills: 1783: radiant eye with star between points of longest rays: NOVA CONSTELLATIO ∗ . ℞ U. S | 1.000 in laurel wreath: LIBERTAS . JUSTITIA . 1783 .: edge engrailed with leaf pattern: silver......$200 00 $100 00 $50 00
Half Dollar, or 500 Mills: 1783: design similar to last design, but 500 in wreath: silver...... 200 00 100 00 50 00
Half Dollar, or 500 Mills: 1783: radiant eye and stars in circle: no legend. ℞ from same die as that of next preceding: silver, 200 00 100 00 50 00
Dime, or 100 Mills: same type as the Dollar, but with value 100 in the wreath: silver......... 200 00 100 00 50 00

Cent, 1783: similar type: no value under U . S in wreath... $1 00 $0 25 $0 10
Cents, 1783: similar type: broad rays........................... 1 00 25 10

	Uncirculated.	Fine.	Good.
Cents, 1785: different dies: *U S* in script: ET added to legend,	$1 00	$0 25	$0 10
Cent, 1785: broad rays, one L. ℞ same as on last: script *U S*...	2 00	1 00	25
Cent, 1786: similar type: small U . s in wreath................	25 00	15 00	10 00

IMMUNE COLUMBIA: Cent, 1785: Liberty seated r. holds balance and flag: IMMUNE COLUMBIA . | 1785 . in ex. ℞ radiant eye: NOVA CONSTELLATIO: milled edge: *silver*......	$50 00	$25 00	$10 00
Cent, 1785: same as last, but in copper: plain edge...........	15 00	10 00	5 00
Cent, 1785: same obv. as last. ℞ NOVA CONSTELLATIO: copper..	20 00	10 00	5 00
Cent, 1785: same obv. as last. ℞ bust of George III. r. CEORCIVS ✳ III. REX . : copper........	15 00	8 00	3 00

                             Uncirculated. Fine. Good.

IMMUNIS COLUMBIA: Cent, 1787: Liberty seated on globe r. holds balance and flag: IMMUNIS COLUMBIA | 1787 in ex. ℞ spread eagle: * E * PLURIBUS * UNUM *: copper, size 17......................$20 00 $10 00 $5 00

Cent, 1787: same as last, but struck on a large planchet: size 19........................ 10 00   5 00   2 00

CONFEDERATIO: Cent, 1785: large stars in radiant circle, short rays: CONFEDERATIO . 1785. ℞ female with bow and arrow stands beside an altar on which is a cap, her foot tramples a crown at base: INIMICA TYRANNIS . AMERICA......... $100 00 $50 00 $25 00

Cent, 1785: small stars in small circle with long rays: CONFED-

	Uncirculated.	Fine.	Good.

ERATIO . 1875. ℞ type similar
to that of last, but AMERICANA
below, and otherwise differently
engraved die.................. $100 00 $50 00 $25 00

Cent, 1785: large stars and circle.
℞ *U S* in script, in wreath:
LIBERTAS ET JUSTITIA, 1785:
similar type to that of Nova
Constellatio Cents........... 50 00   25 00   10 00

Cent, 1786: same obv. as last:
large stars and circle: 1785. ℞
broad heraldic eagle: ✴ E . PLU-
RIBUS UNUM . 1786........... 100 00   50 00   25 00

CONTINENTAL DOLLAR:
1776: sun shining on dial: FU-
GIO at left: MIND YOUR | BUSI-
NESS, in ex.: legend CONTINEN-
TAL CURENCY (*sic*) 1776. ℞ in
radiant circle, AMERICAN CON-
GRESS: inner circle, WE | ARE
| ONE: all surrounded by cir-
cle of thirteen links, each inscribed with name of a State:
silver....................... $150 00 $100 00 $50 00

Dollar, 1776: same dies as last:
comma under N: *brass*....... 25 00   15 00   5 00

Dollar, 1776: from same dies:
pewter...................... 3 00   1 00   50

Dollar, 1776: similar type, but
differently engraved dies: E G

	Uncirculated.	Fine.	Good.

FECIT, over date: sun higher above dial: CURRENCY. ℞ large N in AMERICAN: link inscribed MASSACHS on right of N. HAMP'S: pewter...........$10 00 $3 00 $1 00

Peace token, 1783: Indian Princess before Britannia: dove flying above: St. Paul's l.: FELICITAS: BRITANNIA: ET: AMERICA | MDCCLXXXIII | SEPT. 4. ℞ * after CONGRESS: large N in AMERICAN; pewter............ 10 00 3 00 1 00

Peace token: dove with branch flies toward Indian near tent on sea-shore: TYRANIS . IN . PERPETUUM . ARBEIT . TERRA * . ℞ G in triangle of thirteen stars, surrounded by wedge-like rays in circle: JUVENUS+ CONFEDERATIO + AMERICANA: copper: size 18................ 10 00 3 00 1 00

Fugio, or Franklin Cent.

The first coin issued by authority of the U. S. Government.

	Uncirculated.	Fine.	Good.

Cent: radiant sun over dial: FUGIO. 1787: in ex MIND-YOUR- | BUSINESS. ℞ within serrated band WE | ARE | ONE: UNITED STAT (es) on band: 13 connected links, each with star in centre: GOLD............$100 00 $50 00 $25 00

	Uncirculated.	Fine.	Good.

Cent: same obv. ℞ same as last, but struck before the lettering and band were inserted: *silver*.......................... $25 00 $15 00 $10 00

Cent: sun with numerous fine rays above a dial: no legend. ℞ radiant band inscribed, AMERICAN . CONGRESS. : 13 connected links surrounding: each link bearing the name of a State: eye in centre................. $60 00 $35 00 $25 00

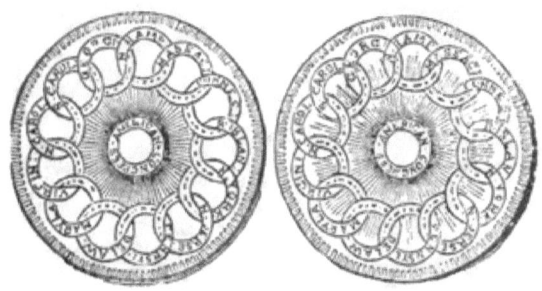

Cent: same obv. ℞ without eye in centre.................... $50 00 $25 00 $15 00
Cent: same obv. ℞ long rays reaching half way through the links 55 00   30 00   20 00
Cent: sun over dial: longer irregular rays: FUGIO. 1787: in ex. MIND-YOUR- | BUSINESS. : in or-

	Uncirculated.	Fine.	Good.
namental letters. ℞ similar to last, with WE | ARE | ONE added in centre: lower parts of links differently ornamented..	50 00	25 00	15 00
Cent: similar obv.: cinquefoil before and after FUGIO, and date: lozenge before MIND and BUSINESS. ℞ WE | ARE | ONE, in centre within circular zone inscribed UNITED above, and STATES below: 13 plain links surrounding................	5 00	3 00	1 00
Cents: same types, but UNITED on left: STATES on right: two with broad or club rays.......	50	10	5
Cents: same types: STATES on left: UNITED on right........	50	10	5

Washington Coins and Tokens.

(Copper, unless otherwise described.)

	Uncirculated.	Fine.	Good.
Cent, 1783: small military bust l.: WASHINGTON & INDEPENDENCE . 1783. ℞ Liberty seated l. holds olive branch and cap on pole: UNITED STATES........	$1 00	$0 25	$0 10
Cent, 1783: same type, but differently engraved dies: large profile.......................	1 00	25	10

	Uncirculated.	Fine.	Good.

Cents, 1783: togated busts l.: legends same as those preceding. ℞ Liberty seated....... $1 00 $0 25 $0 10

Cents, 1785: same types as last: Lincoln's re-strikes in silver, copper and cop-bronzed....... 25   10   5

Cen₁, 1783: similar type but ent'rely different profile......... 2 00   1 00   50

Cent, 1783: arge togated bust l. ℞ value in olive wreath: UNITY STATES OF AMERICA $\frac{1}{100}$: bronze........................ 1 00   50   25

1783 Halfpenny: nude bust r. resembling Geo. III: GEORGIVS . TRIUMPHO. ℞ female behind gate or screen, holds pole and olive branch: VOCE POPOLI: 1783 in ex.................. $1 00 $0 50 $0 25

Cent, 1785: military bust r., with wig: GEN. WASHINGTON. ℞ large stars in radiant circle: CONFEDERATIO . 1785........ 100 00   50 00   25 00

Cent, 1791: military bust l.: WASHINGTON PRESIDENT 1791. ℞ large heraldic eagle with motto-ribbon: ONE CENT above...................... 3 00   2 00   1 00

Cent, 1791: same as last, but thinner planchet: bronzed........ 2 00   1 00   25

1791: similar bust: no date on obv. ℞ small heraldic eagle and clouds, eight stars above: ONE CENT | 1791: edge UNITED STATES OF AMERICA . X...... 3 00   2 00   1 00

	Uncirculated.	Fine.	Good.

Cent, 1791: same as last, but edge inscribed, PAYABLE A MACCLESFIELD LIVERPOOL OR CONGLETON . X.................. $3 00 $2 00 $1 00

Half Dollar, 1792: military bust l.: G. WASHINGTON . PRESIDENT . 1 . 1792. ℞ large heraldic eagle with drooping wings: 13 arrows r.: olive branch with 13 leaves l.: UNITED STATES OF AMERICA: *silver*............$150 00 $100 00 $50 00

Half Dollar, 1792: from similar obv. die as last. ℞ smaller heraldic eagle with upraised wings: 6 arrows r.: 15 leaves on branch l.: 15 stars above: . UNITED STATES OF AMERICA .: *silver*: size 22................ 100 00   50 00   25 00

                      Uncirculated. Fine. Good.

Half Dollar, 1792 : from same dies as last, but edge ornamented with oblong squares and circles : copper: size 23............... $25 00 $10 00 $3 00

Half Dollar, 1792 : from same dies, but plain edge, thicker and smaller planchet: copper: size 21........................ 30 00   15 00   5 00

Cent, 1792 : military bust l. : WASHINGTON PRESIDENT 1792. ℞ heraldic eagle with drooping wings holds 13 arrows and olive branch with 13 leaves in talons: ribbons in beak inscribed UNUM E PLURIBUS: 13 stars above : edge inscribed, UNITED STATES OF AMERICA – * – : GOLD : size 20.............. $200 00 $100 00 $50 00

Cent, 1792 : same as last, but in *silver*...................... . 100 00   50 00   25 00

	Uncirculated.	Fine.	Good.
Cent, 1792: same as last, but in copper: plain edge, smaller planchet: size 19..............	$40 00	$25 00	$10 00
Cent, 1792: same obv. ℞ * GENERAL | OF THE | AMERICAN ARMIES | 1775. | RESIGNED | 1783. | PRESIDENT | OF THE UNITED STATES | 1789: 1775 is under ANA.....................	25 00	15 00	5 00
Cent (n. d.): similar bust: GEO. WASHINGTON BORN VIRGINIA FEB. 11 . 1732. ℞ very similar to that of last, but differently engraved die. 1775 is under ICAN............................	8 00	3 00	1 00

Cent, 1792: large **nude bust** r.: hair bound by ribbon: WASHINGTON PRESIDENT . 1792. ℞ small heraldic eagle, upraised wings: 13 arrows and 14 leaved olive branch in talons: 3 stars each side of head: CENT above: edge inscribed UNITED STATES OF AMERICA . X . X . X	$50 00	$25 00	$10 00
Southampton Halfpenny, 1790: with inscribed edge same as last.........................	2 00	1 00	25
Halfpenny, 1793: military bust l. ℞ ship sailing r.: 1793 in ex.: HALFPENNY above............	2 00	1 00	25

	Uncirculated.	Fine.	Good.

Dollar, 1794 (?): rude military bust l. WASHINGTON PRESIDENT 1794. ℞ standing eagle with extended wings, in olive wreath: UNITED STATES OF AMERICA: copied from rev. of 1795 Dol.: copper: size 25... $5 00 $2 00 $0 50

Halfpenny, 1795: military bust r. G. WASHINGTON. THE FIRM FRIEND TO PEACE & HUMANITY *. ℞ fireplace with grate. LONDON | 1795 below: PAYABLE BY CLARK & HARRIS. 13. WORMWOOD ST. BISHOPSGATE.: edge obliquely milled......... 1 00   50   25

Halfpenny, 1795: same dies as last, but edge inscribed PAYABLE AT LONDON LIVERPOOL OR BRISTOL.— 3 00   2 00   50

Halfpenny, 1795: similar, but differently engraved obv. die: 4 small buttons on coat: queue does not connect with upper part of wig: star at base almost connects both ends of legend...................... 3 00   2 00   50

Penny (n. d.): military bust l.: GEORGE WASHINGTON. ℞ shield surmounted by spread eagle: LIBERTY AND SECURITY:

	Uncirculated.	Fine.	Good.
edge inscribed, AN ASYLUM FOR THE OPPRESS'D OF ALL NATIONS)(:)(..................	$2 00	$1 00	$0 25
Halfpenny, 1795: military bust r. ℞ similar to last, date divided by shield: edge inscribed PAYABLE AT LONDON LIVERPOOL OR BRISTOL..................	2 00	1 00	25
Halfpenny, 1795: same as last, but edge inscribed, LIVERPOOL OR LONDON.......................	2 00	1 00	25
Halfpenny, 1795: same type, but edge inscribed, BIRMINGHAM REDRUTH & SWANSEA.........	2 00	1 00	25
Halfpenny, 1795: same reverse as the preceding. Obv., Hope standing with anchor: . IRISH HALFPENNY . 1795 in ex......	2 00	1 00	25

Cent (n. d.): military bust l., laureated: WASHINGTON above. ℞ similar bust: ONE CENT above..........................	$1 00	$0 50	$0 10

	Uncirculated.	Fine.	Good.
Halfpenny (n. d.): large military bust l. similar to that on 1791 Cents: GEORGEIVS WASHINGTON. ℞ crowned harp, two stars below: NORTH WALES	$5 00	$3 00	$1 00
Halfpenny, (n. d.): same type. ℞ four stars below harp: *fleur-de-lis* on top of crown instead of a star	6 00	3 00	1 00

Perkins' Washington Funeral Medals.

	Uncirculated.	Fine.	Good.
Small military bust l. in wreath of leaf sprays, mostly disconnected, the outside tendrils in pairs: HE IS IN GLORY, THE WORLD IN TEARS. ℞ skull and cross-bones: inscribed in four concentric curved lines: B. FEB. 11 . 1732. GEN. AM. ARMIES, 1775. | RE . 1773, PRES. U. S. AM. '89 . R . '96 . | GEN. ARM. U. S. AM. '98 . | OB. D. 15 . '99: *silver:* size 19	$5 00	$3 00	$1 00
Similar type: but sprays connected; tendrils single. ℞ same as last: *silver:* size 18	3 00	2 00	50
Similar: but struck in white metal,	1 00	50	25
Same obv. ℞ funeral urn inscribed *G W* in script: B . F . 11 . 1732 . G. A. ARM. '75. ℞ . '83. P. U. S. A. '89. | ℞ . '96 G. ARM. U. S. '98 . OB . D . 14 . 1799 .: GOLD: size 19	25 00	15 00	10 00
Same, in *silver*	3 00	2 00	1 00
Same, in copper	2 00	1 00	50
Similar obv., but different die: outer tendrils in pairs: a pellet added between each of the sprays. ℞ similar to last but from different die: no period after s at top of urn: lowest 9 on right does not touch the pedestal: *silver:* size 18	3 00	2 00	1 00

Patterns Issued by U. S. Mint.

	Uncirculated.	Fine.	Good.
Disme, 1792: nude female bust l. with flowing hair: LIBERTY PARENT OF SCIENCE & INDUS.: date below bust. ℞ flying eagle l.: UNITED STATES OF AMERICA | DISME : edge milled : *silver*	$50 00	$20 00	$10 00
Same, 1792 : in *copper*	10 00	5 00	1 05
Half Disme, 1792 : bust of Martha Washington (?) l. : LIB. PAR. OF SCIENCE & INDUSTRY. ℞ flying eagle l. over HALF | DISME | UNI. STATES OF AMERICA: milled edge: silver	5 00	2 00	1 00
Same, 1792 : in *copper : plain edge*,	5 00	2 00	1 00
Silver-Centre, 1792: Cent: nude female bust r.: date below: LIBERTY PARENT OF SCIENCE & INDUST. ℞ ONE | CENT in laurel wreath: below: UNITED STATES OF AMERICA: edge milled : copper with silver plug in centre	50 00	25 00	10 00
Same, 1792: but without silver plug: copper	20 00	8 00	2 00

Birch Cent, 1792: fine female bust r. with curly flowing hair: BIRCH on shoulder, date beneath: LIBERTY PARENT OF SCIENCE & INDUSTRY. * ℞ ONE | CENT in circle in wreath, below: UNITED STATES OF AMERICA: edge inscribed: TO BE ESTEEMED * BE USEFUL * copper: size 20 .... $75 00 $30 00 $15 00

Same, 1792: but with plain edge, 60 00 25 00 10 00

Cent, 1792: nude female bust r. hair tied back: LIBERTY. above: date below. ℞ eagle with upraised wings stands on section of a globe: UNITED STATES OF AMERICA: circle of stars surrounding: edge milled: copper: size 19 .... 100 00 50 00 25 00

MISCELLANEOUS COINS.

Which passed current in the early history of the U. S.

         Uncirculated. Fine. Good.

FLORIDA: Jas. II. Halfpenny, or 1-24 Real: equestrian statue of the King r. ℞ crowned shields of England, Scotland, France and Ireland, chained in cruciform: pewter $3 00 $2 00 $0 50

NEW HAMPSHIRE: Cent, 1766: cedar tree: AMERICAN LIBERTY. ℞ a harp: date r. 1776: cast 10 00 3 00 1 00

Cent, 1776: cedar tree, without ground or roots: AMERICAN LIBERTY. ℞ 1776 over harp: engraved. 10 00 3 00 1 00

	Uncirculated.	Fine.	Good.

RHODE ISLAND: Satirical tokens: British Flag-ship: DE ADMIRAALS FLAG van ADMIRAAL HOWE, 1779. ℞ Patriot soldiers retreating from vicinity of British war-ships to row-boats: D'vlugtende AMERICAANE^n van RHODE YLAND Augt., 1778: bronze or pewter, $1 00 $ 50 $ 10

PITT TOKEN: bust of Wm. Pitt l.: THE . RESTORE^R OF . COMMERCE . 1766 | : NO STAMPS: ℞ ship r.: AMERICA, in field: THANKS . TO . THE . FRIENDS . OF . LIBERTY . AND . TRADE.: copper: size 18.............. $3 00 $1 00 $ 25
Same as last, but tin-plated planchet 2 00 25 10
Similar type, but smaller and differently engraved design: yellow bronze: size 16.......... 5 00 2 00 1 00
¾-faced bust r.: LIBERTATIS VINDEX | GUL: PITT. ℞ hands clasped before liberty-cap on sword: vine wreath: BRITANNIA ET AMERICA JUNCTÆ: yellow bronze: size 21.......... 5 00 2 00 1 00
FRANKLIN PRESS: Halfpenny, 1794: view of his printing press: SIC ORITER DOCTRINA SURGETQUE LIBERTAS. ℞ PAYABLE | AT | THE FRANKLIN | PRESS | LONDON: copper, 1 00 50 10

	Uncirculated.	Fine.	Good.
SHIPS | COLONIES | & | COMMERCE. Obv. ship with U. S. flag r............................	$0 50	$0 20	$0 05
CANADA: Halfpenny, 1794: a river-god with quadrident, reclines on river bank: PONTHON | 1794, in ex.: FERTILITATEM DIVITIAS QUE CIRCUMFERREMUS. ℞ in circle: COPPER | COMPANY | OF UPPER | CANADA: legend, ONE HALF PENNY in large letters: copper............................	20 00	10 00	5 00
Impression from U. S. Revenue embossing die, about 1815: eagle over shield: TEN CENTS below: struck on U. S. cent...	2 00	1 00	25
Columbia Farthings.............	25	10	2
PENNSYLVANIA: Halfpence: 1760: laureated bust r.: VOCE POPULI. ℞ Hibernia seated: HIBERNIA | 1760...............	1 00	50	10
Farthing, 1760: laureated bust r.: VOCE POPULI. ℞ Hibernia seated l.: HIBERNIA | 1760....	5 00	2 00	1 00
Halfpenny, 1736: profile of Geo. III. r.: AUCTORI . . PLEBIS. ℞ crowned harp: HISPANIOLA | 1736........................	1 00	50	10
Philadelphia Shilling: City arms supported by two horses rampant: eagle above. ℞ CORPORATION OF PHILADELPHIA | ONE | SHILLING | TOKEN: Feuchtwanger's composition..	25 00	15 00	5 00
Philadelphia Half Dollar: same obv. as last. ℞ in olive wreath, F.S. | 50 CENTS: same metal as last. The "F.S." is believed to indicate Feuchtwanger's Silver........................	5 00	2 00	1 00

TERRITORIAL GOLD COINS.

The fractional parts of a dollar were made by jewelers for charms and bangles; we give the varieties of shape and date, but there were many sub-varieties of design.

California.

	Uncirculated.	Fine.	Good.
$¼ circular, no date	$0 50	$0 40	$0 30
¼ " 1853-6-9, '64-6-8, '70-1-3-4-6, '80	60	50	40
¼ octagonal, 1852-3-6-9, '60-6-8, '70-1-2-3-6, '80-1	60	50	40
½ circular, 1852-3-9, '66-8, '70-1-3-5-6, '80	90	80	70
½ octagonal, 1852-3-4, '68, '70-1-2-3, '80	90	80	70
1 octagonal, no date	1 50	1 40	1 25
1 octagonal, 1853-4-5-6-7, '60, '70-1-2-4-5	1 50	1 40	1 25
1 circular, 1853-72	1 50	1 25	1 00
1 " 1849, Pacific Company	2 00	1 50	1 25
2.50 head—eagle 1848, Cal. U.S. of A	3 00	2 75	2 50
2.50 head—wreath, 1851, San Francisco, Cal	3 00	2 75	2 50

$5 eagle—1849, California gold without alloy	$5 50	$5 25	$5 00

		Uncirculated.	Fine.	Good.
$5	Columbus Co., 1849. California gold................	$6 00	$5 50	$5 00
5	Indian — eagle, 1849, Cin. Min. & Trad. Co...........	6 50	5 75	5 25
5	T. Dubosq, 1849, S. M. V. California gold.............	6 75	6 00	5 50
5	shield — 1849, Massachusetts & California Co............	7 00	6 00	5 50
5	head—eagle, 1849, Moffatt & Co., S. M. V. Cal..........	6 00	5 50	5 00
5	head—eagle, 1850, Moffatt & Co., S. M. V. Cal..........	6 00	5 50	5 00
5	eagle—liberty cap, 1849, Pacific Co., Cal.	6 00	5 50	5 00
5	head eagle, 1850, Baldwin & Co., S. M. V. Cal..........	6 00	5 50	5 00
5	head—eagle, 1850, Dubosq & Co., S. M. V. Cal..........	6 00	5 50	5 00
5	head—eagle, 1851, Dunbar & Co., S. M. V. Cal..........	6 00	5 50	5 00
5	head—eagle, 1851, Shult & Co., pure California gold....	6 00	5 50	5 00
5	head—eagle, 1852, W. M. & Co., in California..........	6 00	5 50	5 00
5	head—wreath, 1851, S. F., State of California.........	6 00	5 50	5 00
9.43	oblong ingot, Moffatt & Co., 21 7-16 carat...............	11 00	10 00	9 50
10	J. S. O.—31 stars, U. S. of A., California	12 00	11 00	10 50
10	eagle — Miners' Bank, San Francisco..................	12 00	11 00	10 50
10	Moran & Clark, California gold......................	12 00	11 00	10 50
10	Indian—eagle, 1849, Cin. Min. & Trad Co................	12 00	11 00	10 50
10	eagle—liberty cap, 1849, Pacific Co., California........	12 00	11 00	10 50
10	California gold, 1849, Templeton Reid, Assayer	12 00	11 00	10 50
10	head—eagle, 1849, Moffatt & Co., S. M. V. Cal..........	12 00	11 00	10 50
10	horseman—eagle, 1850, Kuner, Baldwin & Co..............	12 00	11 00	10 50
10	head—eagle, 1850, Dubosq & Co., S. M. V. Cal..........	12 00	11 00	10 50

	Uncirculated.	Fine.	Good.
$10 head—eagle, 1851, Baldwin & Co.	$12 00	$11 00	$10 50
10 head—female seated, 1851, S. F., California.	12 00	11 00	10 50
10 eagle—1852, Augustus Humbert, U. S. Assayer.	11 00	10 50	10 00
10 eagle—1852, U. S. Assay office of gold, S. F.	11 00	10 50	10 00
10 head—eagle, 1852, Moffatt & Co., California.	12 00	11 00	10 50
10 head—eagle, 1852, W. M. & Co., S. M. V. Cal.	12 00	11 00	10 50
10 eagle, 1853, U. S. Assay office of gold, S. F.	11 00	10 50	10 00
10 head—eagle, 1855, S. M. V. Cal. gold.	12 00	11 00	10 50
16 oblong ingot, Moffatt & Co., 20¾ carats.	18 00	17 00	16 00
20 eagle—bears, 1850, California gold mines.	25 00	22 00	21 00
20 head—eagle, 1851, Baldwin, S. M. V. Cal.	22 00	21 00	20 00
20 head—female seated, 1851, S. F. Cal.	22 00	21 00	20 00
20 eagle—1853, U. S. Assay office of gold, S. F.	21 00	20 50	20 00
20 head—eagle, 1853, Moffatt & Co., S. F.	22 00	21 00	20 00
20 head—eagle, 1854, Kellogg & Co., S. F.	22 00	21 00	20 00
20 head—eagle, 1855, Kellogg & Co., S. F.	22 00	21 00	20 00
20 head—eagle, 1856, Blake & Co., Sacramento, Cal.	23 00	22 00	21 00
25 California gold, 1849, Templeton Reid, Assayer.	28 00	27 00	26 00
40.07 oblong ingot, 1850, F. D. Kohler, State Aasayer.	43 00	42 00	41 00

California $50, Gold.

	Uncirculated.	Fine.	Good.
$50 octagonal, 1851, name on edge, 50 D. C. 887 thous.	$60 00	$55 00	$52 00
50 octagonal, 1851—Aug. Humbert, etc., near edge.	56 00	53 00	51 00

	Uncirculated.	Fine.	Good.
$50 octagonal, 1852—Aug. Humbert, etc., near edge	$56 00	$53 00	$51 00
50 octagonal, 1851—same, with circles in center	56 00	53 00	51 00
50 octagonal, 1852—U. S. Assay office, S. F. 887 thous	56 00	53 00	51 00
50 octagonal, 1852—U. S. Assay office, S. F. 900 thous	60 00	58 00	56 00
50 circular, 1855, S. F. Cal., W. M. & Co. 900	65 00	60 00	58 00

Colorado.

	Uncirculated.	Fine.	Good.
$2.50 Pike's Peak—J. J. Conway & Co	$2 80	$2 50	$2 50
2.50 head—eagle, 1860, Pike's Peak gold	2 80	2 50	2 50
2.50 head—eagle, 1861, Clark, Gruber & Co	2 80	2 50	2 50
2.50 head—eagle, 1861, same with 2 branches	2 80	2 50	2 50
5 head—eagle, 1860, Pike's Peak gold	6 00	5 50	5 00
5 head—eagle, 1861, Clark, Gruber & Co	6 00	5 50	5 00
5 Pike's Peak, 1860, Denver Assay office	7 00	6 00	5 00
5 machine—eagle, John Parson & Co., Oro City	7 00	6 00	5 00

		Uncirculated.	Fine.	Good.
10	head—eagle, 1861, Clark, Gruber & Co.	$11 00	$10 50	$10 00
10	eagle—peak, 1860, Clark, Gruber & Co.	12 00	11 00	10 50
20	eagle—peak, 1860, Pike's Peak gold	23 00	22 00	20 50
10	head—eagle, 1861, Clark, Gruber & Co.	15 00	12 00	11 00

North Carolina.

		Uncirculated.	Fine.	Good.
$1	Bechtler, Rutherf. 28 G. Carolina dollar	$1 25	$1 10	$1 00
1	A. Bechtler, Carolina gold, 27 G. 21c	1 50	1 35	1 00
1	C. Bechtler, Rutherf. 30 G. ONE	1 30	1 15	1 00
1	C. Bechtler, Rutherf. 30 G. ONE	1 40	1 25	1 00
1	C. Bechtler, Rutherf. 28 G. ONE	1 25	1 10	1 00

$2.50	Bechtler, Rutherf. Ga. gold, 64 G. 22c	$3 00	$2 75	$2 50
2.50	Bechtler, Rutherf. Carolina gold, 67 G. 21c	3 00	2 75	2 50
2.50	C. Bechtler, Rutherf. N. C. gold, 75 G. 20c	3 00	2 75	2 50
5	1834, C. Bechtler at Rutherf. Carolina gold, 140 G. 20c	5 50	5 25	5 00
5	C. Bechtler at Rutherf. Carolina gold, 134 G. 21c	6 00	5 50	5 00
5	C. Bechtler at Rutherf. Georgia gold, 128 G. 22c	5 50	5 25	5 00
5	A. Bechtler, Rutherford, Carolina gold, 134 G. 21c	5 50	5 25	5 00

Oregon.

	Uncirculated.	Fine.	Good.
$5 beaver, 1849, Oregon Exchange Co..................	$6 00	$5 50	$5 00
10 beaver, 1849, Oregon Exchange Co..................	12 00	11 00	10 00

Utah.

	Uncirculated.	Fine.	Good.
$2.50 hands—eye, 1849, Holiness to the Lord..................	$3 00	$2 70	$2 50
5 hands—eye, 1849, Holiness to the Lord..................	6 00	5 50	5 00

	Uncirculated.	Fine.	Good.
$5 hands — eye, 1850, Holiness to the Lord..................	$6 00	$5 50	$5 00
5 bee-hive—lion, Deseret assay office.......................	6 00	5 50	5 00
20 hands—eye, 1849, Holiness to the Lord.....................	23 00	22 00	20 00

Double Eagle or $20.

Authorized by act of Congress, March 3, 1849. Weight 516 grains. Regular coinage commenced 1850. A few were struck off in 1849, and those are the only ones that are rare and quoted at from $1,000 to $5,000. There are no rare dates among the $20 gold pieces of the regular issue, and consequently they do not command a premium except in a strictly uncirculated or proof condition.

1850 to 1858, uncirculated.........................$20 50
1858 to 1890, proofs............................... 20 25

Eagle or $10, Gold.

Authorized by act of Congress April 2, 1792. Weight 270 grains. Coinage commenced 1795. Weight changed by act of June 28, 1834, to 258 grains. None were issued 1802 and 1805 to 1837 inclusive.

	Uncirculated.	Fine.	Good.
1795, 15 stars, 10 l., 5 r...........	$15 00	$12 00	$11 00
1796, 16 stars, 8 l., 8 r............	25 00	18 00	12 00
1797, 16 stars, 12 l., 4 r...........	35 00	25 00	15 00
1797, head l., 16 stars, 10 l., 6 r..	12 00	11 00	10 00
1798, over 1897, large stars, 9 l., 4 r.............................	40 00	35 00	20 00

	Uncirculated.	Fine.	Good.
1798, over 1797, large stars, 7 l., 6 r	$45 00	$35 00	$20 00
1799, large stars, 8 l., 5 r	11 00	10 50	10 00
1800, large stars, 8 l., 5 r	15 00	12 00	11 00
1801, large stars, 8 l., 5 r	12 00	11 00	10 00

1803, large stars, 8 l., 5 r	$12 00	$11 00	$10 00
1804, large stars, 8 l., 5 r	25 00	15 00	11 00
1838, head l. with coronet, proof $35.00	20 00	13 00	11 00
1839, head l. with coronet, proof $30	15 00	12 00	10 50
1840 to 1859	11 00	10 00	10 00
1860 to 1890, proofs	10 50	10 00	10 00

Half Eagle or $5, Gold.

Authorized, act of April 2, 1792. Weight 135 grains. Coinage commenced 1795. Weight changed act of June 28, 1834, to 129 grains. None were issued in 1816 and 1817.

	Uncirculated.	Fine.	Good.
Bust r. with cap: Liberty above. ℞ eagle on olive branch, holding wreath in beak: small eagle.			
1795, 15 stars, 5 facing	$7 00	$6 00	$5 50
1795, obv. as last. ℞ large heraldic eagle with motto, E PLURIBUS UNUM: 16 stars above	40 00	25 00	15 00
1796, over 1795. Small eagle	15 00	12 00	11 00
1797, 15 stars, 5 facing: large eagle	45 00	30 00	20 00
1797, 16 stars, 6 facing: large eagle	13 00	11 00	10 50
1797, 16 stars, 5 facing. ℞ eagle on palm, holds olive wreath in beak	40 00	25 00	15 00
1798, same type as last	50 00	35 00	25 00
1798, large heraldic eagle	7 00	6 00	5 00
1799, large heraldic eagle	8 00	7 00	6 00
1800, large heraldic eagle	6 00	5 00	5 00
1802, over 1801	6 00	5 00	5 00
1803, over 1802	6 00	5 00	5 00
1804	6 00	5 00	5 00
1805	6 00	5 00	5 00
1806, pointed 6; 5 stars r., 8 l.	6 00	5 00	5 00
1806, blunt 6; 6 stars r., 7 l.	7 00	6 00	5 50
1807	6 00	5 00	5 00
1807, new type: cap inscribed LIBERTY	6 00	5 00	5 00
1808, new type: cap inscribed LIBERTY	6 00	5 00	5 00
1809, over 1808	7 00	6 00	5 00
1810, small date	6 00	5 00	5 00
1810, large date	6 00	5 00	5 00
1811	6 00	5 00	5 00
1812	6 00	5 00	5 00
1813	6 00	5 00	5 00
1814, over 1813	8 00	7 00	6 00
1815	200 00	100 00	75 00
1818	6 00	5 00	5 00
1819	35 00	25 00	10 00
1820	10 00	8 00	6 00
1821	30 00	20 00	10 00
1822	500 00	300 00	200 00
1823	9 00	7 00	6 00

	Uncirculated.	Fine.	Good.
1824	$40 00	$30 00	$10 00
1825, over 1821	30 00	20 00	7 00
1825	10 00	8 00	5 00
1826, proof $40.00	25 00	10 00	5 00
1827	40 00	25 00	6 00
1828 over 1827	42 00	30 00	6 00
1829	35 00	20 00	6 00
1829, large date and planchet	45 00	30 00	7 00
1829, small date and planchet	50 00	35 00	10 00
1830	30 00	20 00	6 00
1831	30 00	20 00	6 00
1832	35 00	20 00	6 00
1833	25 00	15 00	6 00
1834, old type	5 25	5 00	5 00
1834, new type: smaller head with band inscribed LIBERTY	5 25	5 00	5 00
1835 to 1858	5 25	5 00	5 00
1858 to 1890, proofs $5.25	5 00	5 00	5 00

Quarter Eagle or $2.50, Gold.

Authorized, act of April 2, 1792. Weight, 67.5 grains. Coinage commenced 1796. Weight changed, Act of June 28, 1834, to 64.5 grains. None issued 1799, 1800, 1801, 1803, 1809 to 1820 inclusive, 1822, 1823, 1828.

	Uncirculated.	Fine.	Good.
Obv. bust of Liberty r., with cap: LIBERTY above ex. date: no stars. R large heraldic eagle, holding label inscribed E PLURIBUS UNUM: stars and clouds above: legend UNITED STATES OF AMERICA.			
1796, obv.: no stars	$15 00	$10 00	$5 00
1796, obv. with 16 stars: proof $50.00	40 00	25 00	15 00
1797, 13 stars. 6 facing	25 00	15 00	10 00
1798, 13 stars, 7 facing	12 00	8 00	5 00

	Uncirculated.	Fine.	Good.
1802, over 1801, 13 stars, 5 facing,	$5 00	$3 00	$2 50
1804, 13 stars, 6 facing............	5 00	3 00	2 50
1805............................	6 00	4 00	3 00
1806, over 1804, 13 stars, 5 facing,	20 00	15 00	10 00
1806, over 1805, 13 stars, 6 facing,	25 00	20 00	15 00
1807, 13 stars, 6 facing............	5 00	3 00	2 50
1808, obv. bust l.: cap inscribed LIBERTY. ℞ heraldic eagle: no stars: ex. 2½d.: 13 stars, 7 facing...........................	5 00	3 00	2 50
1821, 13 stars.....................	15 00	10 00	5 00
1824, over 1821....................	15 00	10 00	5 00
1825.............................	10 00	5 00	3 00
1826, over 1825...................	40 00	25 00	15 00
1827.............................	8 00	5 00	3 00
1829.............................	5 00	3 00	2 50
1830.............................	4 00	2 50	2 50
1831.............................	4 00	2 50	2 50
1832.............................	5 00	3 00	2 00
1833.............................	8 00	5 00	3 00
1834, old type....................	10 00	5 00	3 00
1834, new type: head with band inscribed LIBERTY. ℞ without E PLURIBUS UNUM.........	5 00	2 50	2 50
1835 to 1854.....................	3 00	2 50	2 50
1855 to 1890, proofs $2.75........	2 50	2 50	2 50

$3, Gold.

Authorized, act of February 21, 1853. Weight 77.4 grains. Coinage commenced 1854.

Obv. Indian head l.: band inscribed LIBERTY. ℞ value and date in wreath.

	Uncirculated.	Fine.	Good.
1854.............................	$3 25	$3 00	$3 00
1855.............................	3 25	3 00	3 00
1856.............................	4 00	3 25	3 00

	Proof.	Uncirculated.	Fine.	Good.
1857.....................	$6 00	$3 25	$3 00	$3 00
1858.....................	6 00	3 50	3 25	3 00
1859.....................	5 00	3 10	3 00	3 00
1860.....................	5 00	3 10	3 00	3 00
1861.....................	4 00	3 10	3 00	3 00
1862.....................	3 50	3 10	3 00	3 00

	Proof.	Uncirculated.	Fine.	Good.
1863	$4 00	$3 10	$3 00	$3 00
1864	10 00	4 00	3 25	3 00
1865	5 00	3 10	3 00	3 00
1866	6 00	3 10	3 00	3 00
1867	4 00	3 10	3 00	3 00
1868	5 00	3 25	3 00	3 00
1869	4 00	3 10	3 00	3 00
1870	5 00	3 10	3 00	3 00
1871	6 00	3 10	3 00	3 00
1872	4 00	3 10	3 00	3 00
1873	5 00	3 10	3 00	3 00
1874	3 50	3 10	3 00	3 00
1875	40 00	15 00	10 00	5 00
1876	10 00	6 00	4 00	3 00
1877 to 1890	3 25	3 10	3 00	3 00

Gold Dollars.

Authorized, act of March 3, 1849. Weight, 25.8 grains. Coinage commenced 1849.

Obv. head to l., with coronet inscribed LIBERTY within circle of 13 stars. ℞ legend UNITED STATES OF AMERICA: within wreath, 1 DOLLAR: date.

	Uncirculated.	Fine.	Good.
1849	$1 30	$1 25	$1 15
1850	1 30	1 25	1 15
1851	1 30	1 25	1 15
1852	1 30	1 25	1 15
1853	1 30	1 25	1 15
1854	1 50	1 25	1 15

1854, new type	$1 30	$1 25	$1 15
1855	1 30	1 25	1 15
1856	2 00	1 50	1 25
1856, large head	1 30	1 25	1 15
1856, straight 5	2 00	1 50	1 25

	Uncirculated.	Fine.	Good.
1857	$1 30	$1 25	$1 15
1858	1 30	1 25	1 15
1859	1 30	1 25	1 15
1860	1 30	1 25	1 15
1861	1 30	1 25	1 15
1862	1 30	1 25	1 15
1863	5 00	4 00	3 00
1864	10 00	8 00	5 00
1865	5 00	4 00	3 00
1866	3 00	2 00	1 50
1867	3 00	2 00	1 50
1868	3 00	2 00	1 50
1869	2 50	1 75	1 50
1870	2 00	1 50	1 25
1871	2 00	1 50	1 25
1872	3 00	2 00	1 50
1873	1 30	1 25	1 15
1874	1 30	1 25	1 15
1875	15 00	10 00	5 00
1876	3 00	2 00	1 50
1877	3 00	2 00	1 50
1878	2 50	1 50	1 25
1879	2 00	1 30	1 20
1880 to 1890	1 25	1 15	1 10

U. S. Silver Dollars.

Authorized, act of April 2, 1792. Weight 416 grains. Coinage commenced 1794. Weight changed act January 18, 1837, to 412.5 grains. Coinage discontinued act February 12, 1873. Coinage resumed 1878. None were coined from 1805 to 1835 inclusive, and 1837, 1874 to 1877 inclusive.

	Uncirculated.	Fine.	Good.
Obv. head to r.: flowing hair. ℞ eagle within wreath: legend around the edge HUNDRED CENTS ONE DOLLAR OR UNIT.			
1794	$200 00	$100 00	$25 00
1795, three leaves below each wing,	10 00	3 00	1 50
1795, two leaves below each wing,	5 00	2 00	1 25
Draped bust of Liberty, r. ℞ eagle on clouds.			
1795	5 00	2 00	1 25
1796, small date	5 00	2 00	1 25
1796, large date	6 00	2 50	1 50
1797, seven stars on r	5 00	2 00	1 25
1797, six stars on r	5 00	2 00	1 25
1798, thirteen stars, large lettered rev	6 00	2 50	1 50
1798, fifteen stars, small lettered rev	15 00	8 00	5 00
Bust of Liberty r. ℞ National arms, heraldic eagle.			
1798	4 00	1 50	1 10
1799, over 1798	4 00	1 50	1 10
1799, five stars on r	10 00	6 00	4 00
1799, six stars on r	4 00	1 50	1 10
1800	4 00	1 50	1 10
1801	10 00	3 00	1 50
1802, over 1801	10 00	3 00	1 50
1802	10 00	3 00	1 50
1803, large 3	8 00	2 00	1 25
1803, small 3	9 00	3 00	1 50
1804	$600 00	$300 00	$200 00

NOTE: There are numerous counterfeits bearing the date of 1804. They are generally made out of the 1801, which bears a close resemblance to the 1804, by cutting out the 1 in the date and inserting a 4 in its place. Any scratches or depressions about the date are sure indications that the coin is false. There are also re-strikes, made with the original dies but at a later date, and as they did not have the collar the lettering around the edge is irregular, as it was put on by hand afterwards.

	Uncirculated.	Fine.	Good.
Liberty seated. ℞ flying eagle l.			
1836, C. Gobrecht, F on base.....	$10 00	$6 00	$3 00
1836, C. Gobrecht below base....	30 00	20 00	15 00
1836, C. Gobrecht on base : ℞ no stars............................	50 00	30 00	20 00

	Uncirculated.	Fine.	Good.
1838, stars on obv. only, milled edge	$50 00	$30 00	$20 00
1838, stars on ℞ like on 1836, plain edge	55 00	30 00	20 00
1839, stars on ℞ like 1836, plain edge	50 00	30 00	20 00
1839, stars on obv. only, milled edge	30 00	20 00	10 00

Liberty seated r. ℞ eagle standing.

1840		$2 00	$1 00	$1 00
1841		2 00	1 00	1 00
1842		2 00	1 00	1 00
1843		2 00	1 00	1 00
1844		2 00	1 00	1 00
1845		2 00	1 00	1 00
1846, New Orleans mint first coins dollars		2 00	1 00	1 00
1847		2 00	1 00	1 00
1848		2 00	1 00	1 00
1849		2 00	1 00	1 00
1850		2 00	1 00	1 00

	Proof.	Uncirculated.	Fine.	Good.
1851	$45 00	$30 00	$20 00	$15 00
1852	45 00	30 00	20 00	15 00
1853	8 00	5 00	2 00	1 50
1854	10 00	6 00	3 00	2 00
1855	15 00	4 00	2 00	1 50
1856	6 00	3 00	2 00	1 50
1857	4 00	3 00	2 00	1 50

	Proof.	Uncirculated.	Fine.	Good.
1858	$35 00	$30 00	$20 00	$15 00
1859, San Francisco mint first coins dollars	2 00	1 50	1 00	1 00
1860	2 00	1 50	1 00	1 00
1861, New Orleans mint suspends coinage Jan. 26	2 00	1 25	1 00	1 00
1862	1 50	1 10	1 00	1 00
1863	1 50	1 10	1 00	1 00
1864	2 00	1 50	1 00	1 00
1865	1 50	1 10	1 00	1 00
1866	1 50	1 10	1 00	1 00
1866, with IN GOD WE TRUST (on all following)	1 50	1 10	1 00	1 00
1867	1 50	1 10	1 00	1 00
1868	1 50	1 10	1 00	1 00
1869	1 50	1 10	1 00	1 00
1870, Carson City mint first coins dollars	1 50	1 10	1 00	1 00
1871	1 50	1 10	1 00	1 00
1872	1 50	1 10	1 00	1 00
1873	1 50	1 10	1 00	1 00

The new series are called the Bland Dollar, and Miss Annie L. Williams, a Philadelphia school-teacher, represents the French profile of Liberty. There is an interesting story connected with the way in which Miss Williams' profile came to be used on the Bland Dollar. In the winter of 1877-78 G. T. Morgan, the designer, was working on sketches for the imprint of the then new silver dollar. Previous to this there had been no dollars coined for five years. Prof. Thomas Eakins, then of the Academy of the Fine Arts, advised him to use a ife study, and introduced him to Miss Annie L. Williams, a schoolteacher, living at Thirteenth and Spring Garden streets. Miss Williams, who possessed strikingly classical features, consented to sit for the drawing, and her profile was used to complete the design.

	Proof.	Uncirculated.	Fine.	Good.
1878, three leaves on olive branch	$2 00	$1 10	$1 00	$1 00
1878, nine leaves on olive branch: eight tail feathers	1 50	1 10	1 00	1 00
1878, seven tail feathers	1 50	1 10	1 00	1 00
1879, New Orleans mint resumes operations Feb. 20	1 50	1 10	1 00	1 00
1880	1 50	1 00	1 00	1 00
1881	1 50	1 00	1 00	1 00
1882	1 50	1 00	1 00	1 00
1883	1 25	1 00	1 00	1 00
1884	1 25	1 00	1 00	1 00
1885	1 25	1 00	1 00	1 00
1886	1 25	1 00	1 00	1 00
1887	1 25	1 00	1 00	1 00
1888	1 25	1 00	1 00	1 00
1889	1 25	1 00	1 00	1 00
1890	1 25	1 00	1 00	1 00

Trade Dollars.

Authorized, act of February 12, 1873. Weight 420 grains. Coinage commenced in 1873. Repudiated in 1884. Redeemed, 1887. Struck at Philadelphia, San Francisco and Carson City mints.

	Proof.	Uncirculated.	Fine.
1873	$1 25	$1 00	$0 75

	Proof.	Uncirculated.	Fine.
1874	$1 25	$ 80	$ 75
1875	1 25	80	75
1876	1 25	80	75
1877	1 10	80	75
1878	1 10	80	75
1879	1 10	80	75
1880	1 10	80	75
1881	1 10	80	75
1882	1 10	80	75
1883	1 10	80	75

U. S. Silver Half Dollars.

Authorized, act of April 2, 1792. Weight 208 grains. Coinage commenced 1794. Weight changed, acts of January 18, 1837, to 206.25 grains, February 21, 1853, to 192 grains, February 12, 1873, to 192.9 grains. None issued in 1798, 1799, 1800 and 1816.

	Uncirculated.	Fine.	Good.
Profile of Liberty r. ℞ eagle in wreath.			
1794	$15 00	$5 00	$1 00
1795	3 00	1 00	65
1795, double date: three leaves below each wing	5 00	2 00	1 00
1795, double date, two leaves below each wing	3 00	1 00	65
Bust of Liberty r. ℞ eagle on clouds: ½ below.			
1796, fifteen stars	100 00	50 00	20 00
1796, sixteen stars	110 00	55 00	22 00
1797	100 00	50 00	20 00

Bust of Liberty r. ℞ National arms.

	Uncirculated.	Fine.	Good.
1801	$10 00	$5 00	$2 00
1802	10 00	5 00	2 00
1803, large 3	2 00	1 00	50
1803, small 3	3 00	2 00	50
1805, over 1804	4 00	2 00	50
1805	1 00	55	50
1806, over 1805	4 00	2 00	50
1806, over 1809: (6 first sunk inverted)	5 00	2 50	1 00
1806, figure thus, 6 : wide date,	1 00	65	50
1806, figure thus, 6	1 00	65	50
1806, figure thus, 6 : no stem to olive branch	1 50	75	50
1807	1 50	75	50

Bust of Liberty l., with Phrygian cap. ℞ standing eagle.

	Uncirculated.	Fine.	Good.
1807, large stars	1 25	60	50
1807, small stars	1 00	60	50
1807, ℞ 50c. over 20	2 00	1 00	75
1808, over 1807	1 00	60	50
1808	1 00	60	50
1809	1 00	60	50
1810, large date	1 00	60	50
1810, small, thin date	2 00	1 00	75
1811, small 8	1 00	60	50
1811, large 8	1 25	75	50
1811, punctuated date, 18.11	1 25	75	50
1812, over 1811, small date	1 25	75	50
1812, large date	1 00	75	50
1813	1 00	60	50
1813, ℞ INN cut between 50—c	2 25	1 55	50
1814, over 1813	1 00	1 00	75
1814	1 00	1 00	50
1815, over 1812 (always),	5 00	3 55	1 50
1817, over 1813	1 00	55	50
1817, punctuated date, 181.7	1 25	75	50
1817	1 00	60	50
1818, over 1817	1 00	60	50
1818	1 00	55	50
1819, over 1818, small 9	1 00	60	50
1819, over 1818, large 9	1 25	75	50
1819	1 00	55	50

	Uncirculated.	Fine.	Good.
1820, over 1819	$1 00	$0 60	$0 50
1820, large 2	1 00	60	50
1820, small 2	1 00	60	50
1821	75	50	50
1822	75	50	50
1823	75	50	50
1824, over 1822-21-20-19, parts of each figure showing	1 00	60	50
1824, over 1821	75	50	50
1824	60	50	50
1825	60	50	50
1826	60	50	50
1827, over 1826	75	55	50
1827, curled 2	70	55	50
1827, square base 2	60	50	50
1828, large date, curled 2	75	55	50
1828, small date, square base 2	75	50	50
1829, over 1827	1 00	75	50
1829	60	50	50
1830, large O in date	75	55	50
1830, small o in date	60	50	50
1831	60	50	50
1832, large letters in legend	75	55	50
1832, small letters in legend	55	50	50
1833	55	50	50
1834, large date and letters	55	50	50
1834, large date and small letters	55	50	50
1834, small date and small letters	55	50	50
1835	55	50	50
1836, last year of lettered edge	55	50	50

Bust Liberty l., seven stars r. ℞ no motto over eagle: edge milled.

	Uncirculated.	Fine.	Good.
1836, milled edge	5 00	2 00	1 00
1837	55	50	50
1838, o under bust	$15 00	$5 00	$2 00
1838, HALF DOL. below eagle (New Orleans m.m. first occurs)	55	50	50
1838, Liberty seated r. ℞ of 1839	25 00	10 00	5 00
1838, Liberty seated. ℞ of 1837	25 00	10 00	5 00
1839	55	50	50
1839, without sleeve at right elbow,	55	50	50
1839, with sleeve at right elbow	1 00	75	50
1839, old type	55	55	50

Liberty seated r. ℞ standing eagle.

83

	Uncirculated.	Fine.	Good.
1840, large letters in legend	$2 00	$1 00	$0 75
1840, small letters in legend	55	50	50
1841	65	55	50
1842, large date	60	50	50
1842, small date	65	50	50
1843	55	50	50
1844	60	55	50
1845, over 1841	1 00	75	55
1845	75	55	50
1846, over 1849	1 50	1 00	55
1846, large date	75	55	50
1846, small date	55	50	50
1847, over 1846	1 50	1 00	55
1847	55	50	50
1848	65	55	50
1849	65	55	50
1850	70	55	50
1851	1 00	60	50
1852	2 00	1 50	1 00
1853, without arrows at side of date and without rays back of the eagle: same type as preceding	10 00	5 00	3 00

NOTE: See illustrations among the quarter dollars of the same year.

1853, with arrow-heads at date. ℞ with rays (Act Feb. 21, reduced weight to 192 grains)	$0 55	$0 50	$0 50
1854	55	50	50
1855, San Francisco m.m. first occurs	55	50	50
1856, without arrow-heads at date: *like all following, exceptions noted*	55	50	50

	Uncirculated.	Fine.	Good.
1856, twice engraved date	$1 00	$0 75	$0 55
1857	55	50	50
1858	55	50	50

	Proof.	Uncirculated.	Fine.
1859	$0 70	$0 50	$0 50
1860	70	50	50
1861, New Orleans Mint suspends coinage May 30, Confederate Govt. coining over 2,000,000 pieces after the seizure, Jan. 26	70	50	50
1862	75	50	50
1863	75	50	50
1864	80	50	50
1865	75	50	50
1866, without IN GOD WE TRUST,	3 00	2 00	1 00
1866, with IN GOD WE TRUST, over eagle (on all following)	75	50	50
1867	75	50	50
1868	75	50	50
1869	70	50	50
1870, Carson City *m.m.* first occurs,	70	50	50
1871	70	50	50
1872	70	50	50
1873	75	55	50
1873, with arrow-heads at date	70	50	50
1874, with arrow-heads at date	65	50	50
1875	60	50	50
1876	60	50	50
1877	65	50	50
1878	60	50	50
1879	65	50	50
1880	65	50	50
1881	65	50	50
1882	65	50	50
1883	65	50	50
1884	65	50	50
1885	65	50	50
1886	65	50	50
1887	65	50	50
1888	65	50	50
1889	65	50	50
1890	65	50	50

Quarter Dollars.

Authorized, act of April 2, 1792. Weight, 104 grains. Coinage commenced, 1796. Weight changed, acts of January, 18, 1837, to 103.-125 grains; February 21, 1853, to 96 grains; February 12, 1873, to 96.45 grains. None issued in 1797 to 1804, 1808 to 1814, inclusive, 1816, 1817, 1826, 1829, 1830.

	Uncirculated.	Fine.	Good.
Bust of Liberty r. ℞ eagle on clouds.			
1796	$15 00	$5 00	$2 00
Bust of Liberty r.: 13 stars. ℞ National arms.			
1804	15 00	5 00	2 00
1805	3 00	50	25
1806, over 1805	3 00	50	25
1806	1 00	30	25
1807	10 00	2 00	30
Bust of Liberty l., with Phrygian cap. ℞ standing eagle, motto above.			
1815	2 00	50	25
1818	1 00	25	25
1819, large 9	2 00	30	25
1819, small 9	3 00	50	30
1820, large O in date	2 00	30	25
1820, small o in date	2 00	30	25
1821	2 00	30	25

	Uncirculated.	Fine.	Good.
1822	$3 00	$0 40	$0 25
1822, ℞ "25" over "50 5"	3 00	40	25
1823, over 1822 (always)	100 00	50 00	25 00
1824, over 1822	10 00	5 00	1 00
1824	8 00	3 00	50
1825, over 1823 and 1822 (showing why the 1823 was never restruck)	2 00	50	25
1825, over 1824	3 00	75	25
1827 (those showing rusted die are re-strikes)	100 00	50 00	25 00
1828	1 00	25	25
1828, ℞ "25" over "50 5"	2 00	50	25

Small bust of Liberty l. ℞ small eagle: no motto.

	Uncirculated.	Fine.	Good.
1831, large letter in legend: large 25	1 00	30	25
1831, small letters in legend: small 25	1 00	30	25
1832	1 00	30	25
1833	1 00	30	25
1834		30	25	25
1835		30	25	25
1836		75	25	25
1837		50	25	25
1838		50	25	25

Liberty seated r. ℞ smaller eagle: quar. dol.

	Uncirculated.	Fine.	Good.
1838		50	25	25
1839		50	25	25
1840, without sleeve at right elbow (New Orleans m.m. first occurs)		50	25	25
1840, with sleeve at right elbow	1 00	30	25
1841		50	25	25
1842, large date		30	25	25
1843		50	25	25
1844	1 00	30	25
1845		50	25	25
1846, perfect date		60	30	25
1846, twice engraved date	1 00	30	25
1847		50	25	25
1848	1 00	50	25
1848, twice engraved date	1 25	75	50
1849		60	30	25

	Uncirculated.	Fine.	Good.
1850	$0 60	$0 30	$0 25
1851	60	30	25
1852	1 00	50	25

1853, without arrow-heads at date.
 ℞ no rays.................... $8 00 $3 00 $1 00

NOTE: There are numerous counterfeit coins of this date. Some are made out of the 1853 with arrows and with rays, simply by punching the objectionable arrow heads and rays out of sight. Others are made out of the 1858 quarter, by changing the 8 into a 3. All these frauds can easily be detected by weighing them. The genuine 1853 quarters without arrows weigh 103.125 grains; those with arrows only 96 grains. The same frauds are also practiced with the 1853 half dollars.

1853, with arrow-heads at date. ℞ with rays (act Feb. 21, reduced weight to 96 grains)...	$0 30	$0 25	$0 25
1854..........................	30	25	25
1855, San Francisco *m.m.* first occurs......................	30	25	25

	Uncirculated.	Fine.	Good.
1856, without arrow-heads at date (and all hereafter, exceptions noted)	$0 30	$0 25	$0 25
1857	30	25	25

	Proof.	Uncirculated.	Fine.
1858	$0 50	$0 25	$0 25
1859	40	25	25
1860, last date coined in New Orleans mint	40	25	25
1861	40	25	25
1862	35	25	25
1863	40	25	25
1864	45	25	25
1865	45	25	25
1866, without IN GOD WE TRUST	3 00	1 00	50
1866, IN GOD WE TRUST, over eagle (on all following)	40	25	25
1867	40	25	25
1868	40	25	25
1869	35	25	25
1870, Carson City *m.m.* first occurs	35	25	25
1871	35	25	25
1872	35	25	25
1873	35	25	25
1874 to 1890	35	25	25

Twenty Cent Pieces.

Authorized, act of March 5, 1875. Weight, 77.16 grains. Regular coinage commenced in 1875; a few pattern pieces were struck off in 1874. Coinage discontinued act of May 2, 1878.

Liberty seated r. ℞ eagle with arrows on l.

	Proof.	Uncirculated.	Fine.
1875 (Issued at Phila., San Fran. and Carson City)	$0 30	$0 20	$0 20
1876 (Issued at Phila. and Carson City)	50	30	20
1877 (Issued at Phila., only proofs)	1 00	75	50
1878 (Issued at Phila., only proofs)	1 00	75	50

Dimes, or Ten Cent Pieces.

Authorized, act of April 2, 1792. Weight 41.6 grains. Coinage commenced in 1796. Weight changed, acts January 18, 1837, to 41.25 grains; February 21, 1853, to 38.4 grains; February 12, 1873, to 38.58 grains. None issued 1799, 1806, 1808, 1810, 1812, 1813, 1815 to 1819, inclusive, and 1826.

	Uncirculated.	Fine.	Good.
Bust of Liberty r. ℞ eagle on clouds.			
1796	$5 00	$3 00	$1 00
1797, 13 stars	15 00	5 00	2 00
1797, 16 stars	25 00	10 00	3 00
Bust Liberty r. ℞ National arms.			
1798, over 1797: thirteen stars	13 00	3 00	1 00
1798	10 00	3 00	1 00
1800	15 00	5 00	2 00
1801	10 00	3 00	1 00
1802	15 00	5 00	2 00
1803	10 00	3 00	1 00
1804	25 00	10 00	3 00
1805	1 00	50	25
1807	3 00	1 00	50

Bust Liberty l., with Phrygian cap. ℞ eagle below motto.

	Uncirculated.	Fine.	Good.
1809	$5 00	$2 00	$1 00
1811, over 1809	5 00	2 00	1 00
1814, large date	2 00	1 00	15
1814, small date	3 00	1 00	20
1820, large O in date	1 00	25	15
1820, small o in date	1 00	20	10
1821, large date	1 00	20	10
1821, small date	1 00	20	10
1822	10 00	5 00	1 00
1823, over 1822: large E's in legend	1 00	25	15
1823, over 1822: small E's in legend	2 00	50	25
1824, over 1822: large E's in legend	1 00	25	15
1825	50	15	10
1827	1 00	50	
1828, large date	5 00	1 00	50
1828, small date	30	10	10
1829, large 10C. on ℞	30	10	10
1829, small 10C. on ℞	30	10	10
1830	15	10	10
1831	15	10	10
1832	15	10	10
1833	15	10	10
1834, large 4 in date	15	10	10
1834, small 4 in date	20	10	10
1835	15	10	10
1836	20	10	10
1837	25	10	10

Liberty seated r. ℞ ONE DIME in wreath.

1837, without stars: large date, 3,	25	10	10
1837, without stars: small date, 3,	25	10	10
1838, without stars: New Orleans Mint only	1 00	15	10
1838, with stars	20	10	10
1839	25	10	10
1840	30	10	10
1840, with sleeve at right elbow,	50	10	10
1841	30	10	10
1842	30	10	10
1843	30	10	10
1844	50	10	10
1845	20	10	10

	Uncirculated.	Fine.	Good.
1846	$2 00	$0 75	$0 25
1847	20	10	10
1848	50	10	10
1849	20	10	10
1850	15	10	10
1851	15	10	10
1852	20	10	10
1853	15	10	10
1853, with arrow-heads at date (act Feb. 21 reduces weight to 38⅜ grains)	15	10	10
1854	15	10	10
1855	20	10	10
1856, large date, without arrow-heads at date (same on all following, exceptions noted),	25	10	10
1856, small date (San Francisco m.m. first occurs)	15	10	10
1857	15	10	10

	Proof.	Uncirculated.	Fine.
1858	$0 25	$0 10	$0 10
1859	15	10	10
1859, with ℞ of 1860	1 00	50	25
1860, with stars, San Francisco mint only	1 00	50	25
Liberty seated r., legend surrounding. , ℞ wreath of corn, cotton, etc.			
1860, last date of New Orleans mint	15	10	10
1861	15	10	10
1862 to 1890	15	10	10

Half Dimes, or 5 Cents.

Authorized, act of April 2, 1792. Weight 20.8 grains. Coinage commenced 1794. Weight changed, acts of January 18, 1837, to 20.625 grains, February 12, 1853, 19.2 grains. Coinage discontinued, act of February 12, 1873. None coined in 1798, 1799, 1801, 1806 to 1823 inclusive.

	Uncirculated.	Fine.	Good.

Profile of Liberty r. ℞ eagle in wreath.

	Uncirculated	Fine	Good
1794	$10 00	$3 00	$1 00
1795	2 00	1 00	50

Bust of Liberty r. ℞ eagle on clouds.

1796	12 00	4 00	1 00
1797, sixteen stars	4 00	1 00	30
1797, fifteen stars	5 00	2 00	50
1797, thirteen stars	6 00	2 50	75

Bust of Liberty r. ℞ National arms.

1800	1 00	50	25
1800, LIBEKTY (!)	2 00	1 00	50
1801	10 00	3 00	1 00
1802	200 00	100 00	50 00
1803	12 00	4 00	1 00
1805	25 00	10 00	3 00

Bust of Liberty l., with Phrygian cap. ℞ eagle below motto.

1829	25	5	5
1830	25	5	5
1831	25	5	5
1832	25	5	5
1833	20	5	5
1834	20	5	5
1835, large date: large 5C. on ℞	50	20	10
1835, large date: small 5C. on ℞	20	5	5
1835, small date: small 5C. on ℞	20	5	5
1835, small date: large 5C. on ℞	50	20	10
1836, small 5C. on ℞	25	5	5
1836, large 5C. on ℞	50	15	10
1837	20	5	5

Liberty seated r. ℞ HALF DIME in wreath.

1837, without stars: large date	20	5	5
1837, without stars: small date	20	5	5
1838, without stars: New Orleans Mint only	75	50	10
1838, with stars	15	5	5
1839	15	5	5
1840	20	5	5
1840, with sleeve at right elbow	50	25	10

	Uncirculated.	Fine.	Good.
1841	$0 25	$0 05	$0 05
1842	50	15	5
1843	30	10	5
1844	50	5	5
1844, twice engraved date	55	5	5
1845	15	5	5
1845, twice engraved date	30	5	5
1846	3 00	1 00	50
1847	10	5	5
1848, large date	1 00	25	10
1848, small date	10	5	5
1849 over 1848	1 00	25	10
1849	10	5	5
1850	10	5	5
1851	10	5	5
1852	10	5	5
1853	15	5	5
1853, with arrow-heads at date (Act of Feb. 21 reduces weight to 19½ grains)	10	5	5
1854	10	5	5
1855	10	5	5
1856, without arrow-heads at date (all following same)	10	5	5
1857	10	5	5

	Proof.	Uncirculated.	Fine.
1858	$0 15	$0 05	$0 05
1859	10	5	5
1860	25	10	5

Liberty seated r., legend surrounding. ℞ wreath of corn, cotton, etc.

1860, last date of New Orleans mint	10	5	5
1861	10	5	5
1862	10	5	5
1863, San Francisco m. m. first occurs	15	5	5
1864	25	5	5
1865	20	5	5
1866	15	5	5
1867	15	5	5
1868	10	5	5
1869	10	5	5

	Proof.	Uncirculated.	Fine.
1870	$0 10	$0 05	$0 05
1871	10	5	5
1872	10	5	5
1873	10	5	5

Silver Three Cent Pieces.

Authorized, act of March 3, 1851. Weight, 12.373 grains. Coinage commenced 1851. Weight changed, act of March 3, 1853, to 11.92 grains. Coinage discontinued act of February 12, 1875.

	Proof.	Uncirculated.	Fine.
Shield on six-pointed star. ℞ III within C.			
1851 (only year of New Orleans *m. m.*)	$0 10	$0 03	$0 03
1852	25	3	3
1853	10	3	3
Similar, with two additional outlines to star. ℞ olive branch above, three arrows below III.			
1854	50	25	3
1855	2 00	1 00	5
1856	1 00	10	3
1857	50	10	3
1858	50	5	3
Similar, but smaller letters, and only one outline around star.			
1859	10	3	3
1860	10	3	3
1861	10	3	3
1862	10	3	3
1863	25	3	3

	Uncirculated.	Fine.	Good.
1864	$ 50	$0 03	$0 03
1865	25	3	3
1866	25	3	3
1867	20	3	3
1868	20	3	3
1869	20	3	3
1870	15	3	3
1871	15	3	3
1872	15	3	3
1873, coinage ceased April 1st	20	3	3

Five Cents, Nickel.

Authorized, act of May 16, 1866. Weight 77.16 grains. Coinage commenced 1866.

Shield surmounted by cross and olive branches. ℞ 5 in circle of alternate stars and rays.

	Proof.	Uncirculated.
1866, large date, small motto	$0 50	$0 15
1866, small date, large motto	25	10
1867	50	15

Similar, but rays omitted.

1867	10	5
1868	10	5
1869, small date	25	15
1869, large date	10	5
1870	10	5
1871	15	5
1872	10	5
1873	10	5
1874	10	5

	Proof.	Uncirculated.
1875	$0 10	$0 05
1876	10	5
1877, proofs only	50	5
1878	10	5
1879	10	5
1880	10	5
1881	10	5
1882	10	5
1883	10	5

Profile of Liberty l., with coronet. ℞ v in wreath of cotton and corn.

1883, without word CENTS: motto below,	$0 10	$0 05
1883, with word CENTS: motto above,	7	5
1884	7	5
1885	7	5
1886	7	5
1887	7	5
1888	7	5
1889	7	5
1890	7	5

Three Cents, Nickel.

Authorized, act of March 3, 1865. Weight, 30 grains. Coinage commenced, 1865. Discontinued, 1890.

Profile of Liberty l., with coronet. ℞
III in olive wreath.

                                            Proof. Uncirculated.

	Proof	Uncirculated
1865	$0 15	$0 03
1865, copper	25	5
1866	5	3
1867	5	3
1867, copper	25	5
1868	5	3
1869	5	3
1870	5	3
1871	5	3
1872	5	3
1873	5	3
1874	5	3
1875	5	3
1876	5	3
1877	25	5
1878	5	3
1879	5	3
1880	5	3
1881	5	3
1882	5	3
1883	5	3
1884	5	3
1885	5	3
1886	5	3
1887, over 1886	5	3
1887	5	3
1888	5	3
1889	5	3
1890	5	3

Two Cents, Bronze.

Authorized, act of April 22, 1864. Weight, 96 grains. Coinage commenced, 1864. Discontinued, 1873.

Shield on crossed arrows surmounted by scroll and wreath. ℞ value in wheat wreath.

	Proof.	Uncirculated.
1864, small motto	$0 50	$0 05
1864, large motto	25	5
1864, large motto, copper-nickel	50	5
1865	15	3
1865, silver-copper	50	3
1865, copper-nickel	50	3
1866	10	2
1867	10	2
1868	5	2
1869	5	2
1870	5	2
1871	5	2
1872	10	3
1873, coinage discontinued April 1st	25	5

Cents, Copper.

Authorized, act of July 6, 1787. Coined for the United States by James Jarvis, of New Haven, Conn. These are the so-called Fugio or Franklin cents. The regular large copper cents were authorized, act of April 2, 1792. Weight 264 grains. Weight changed, act of January 14, 1793, to 203 grains. Weight changed, act of March 3, 1795, to 168 grains. Coinage commenced in 1793; discontinued, 1857. None were issued in 1815.

	Uncirculated.	Fine.	Good.

1793 Cent: profile of Liberty r.: period after LIBERTY . and date. ℞ ONE | CENT | $\frac{1}{100}$ in circle of 13 links: UNITED STATES OF AMERICA: bars and flowering strawberry vine on edge........................ $50 00 $15 00 $2 00

1793, same type, but different dies: no periods: date curved and widely spaced.... .... 50 00   15 00   2 00

1793, similar type: AMERI. on ℞, $100 00 $25 00 $5 00

1793, different profile of Liberty: long, thin locks of hair: long point to bust: date and LIBERTY smaller: strawberry sprig of three leaves and a blossom,

	Uncirculated.	Fine.	Good.

over date. ℞ ONE | CENT in wreath of laurel and strawberry leaves: UNITED STATES OF AMERICA $\frac{1}{100}$: vine and bars on edge.................. $100 00 $25 00 $5 00

1793, similar type: larger figures in date, over which is a narrow-leaved olive sprig of three leaves: border of pearls. ℞ long, broad stems to wreath: vine and bars on edge......... $30 00 $10 00 $1 00

1793, same type: leaves of olive sprig point to r.: stem almost touches top of 9. ℞ die differ-

	Uncirculated.	Fine.	Good.
ent from next preceding: ONE HUNDRED FOR A DOLLAR, on edge....................	$50 00	$15 00	$2 00
1793, differently engraved profile: hair thicker: broad-leaved olive sprig over 9 in date. ℞ legend almost touches the circle of pearls: vine and bars on edge.....................	50 00	15 00	2 00
1793, similar profile: broadleaved olive sprig over 7 in date: large letters in LIBERTY. ℞ same die as that of next preceding: vine and bars on edge.....................	40 00	10 00	1 00

1793, bust of Liberty r., with cap on pole. ℞ value in olive wreath: ONE HUNDRED FOR A DOLLAR, on edge: size 18....	$55 00	$20 00	$3 00
1793, same dies: size 17½........	50 00	15 00	2 00
1794, double chin...............	10 00	1 00	25
1794, many haired..............	10 00	1 00	25
1794, separated date............	12 00	1 00	30
1794, fallen 4...................	11 00	1 00	25
1794, short bust.................	10 00	1 00	25
1794, Patagonian................	10 00	1 00	25
1794, marred field..............	10 00	1 00	25
1794, plica.....................	12 00	2 00	50

1794, double chin: same obv. die as No. 1. ℞ quite different from that of No. 1: N E of ONE

	Uncirculated.	Fine.	Good.
are widely spaced, not joined at tops as in No. 1: legend more distant from border	$25 00	$5 00	$1 00
1795, nude bust r., with cap and pole. ℞ ONE | CENT high in wreath: ONE HUNDRED FOR A DOLLAR, on edge	10 00	1 00	25
1795, similar, but different dies: wreath terminates in single leaves: plain edge	5 00	50	10
1795, same obv. die. ℞ value evenly spaced in a wreath formed of groups of three leaves, except at top	5 00	50	10
1795, 5 in date not touching bust. ℞ value evenly spaced: leaves in pairs	6 00	1 00	25
1795, the so-called Jefferson head: die work entirely different from any other of the series	10 00	2 00	1 00
1796, nude bust r., with cap on pole	25 00	5 00	1 00
1796, same type: open mouth	10 00	1 00	25

1796, draped bust r.: 1 and 6 touch hair and bust: wide milling on border	$15 00	$2 00	$0 50
1796, same type: different dies: date not touching bust. ℞ ONE | CENT much closer together	10 00	1 00	25

	Uncirculated.	Fine.	Good.
1796, LIBERTY	$10 00	$2 00	$1 00
1797, indented edge	5 00	50	5
1797, plain edge	2 00	15	5
1797, knobless 9	8 00	1 15	25
1797, stemless wreath	2 00	20	10
1798, over 1797	2 00	10	5
1798, large date, milled edge	1 50	10	5
1798, large date, plain edge	1 00	5	2
1798, small date, plain edge	50 00	10 00	2 00
1799, over 1798	60 00	15 00	3 00

1799	$60 00	$15 00	$3 00
1800, over 1790	1 00	5	2
1800, over 1798	1 00	10	5
1800, over 1799	1 00	5	2
1800, perfect date	1 00	5	2
1801, $\frac{1}{000}$ IINITED: *one* stem to wreath	2 00	50	25
1801, $\frac{1}{000}$	1 00	5	2
1801, $\frac{1}{100}$ over $\frac{1}{000}$	1 00	5	2
1801, perfect date	1 00	5	2
1802, $\frac{1}{000}$	2 00	10	2
1802, $\frac{1}{100}$ over $\frac{1}{000}$	1 00	5	2
1802, one stem to wreath	1 00	5	2
1802, stemless wreath	1 00	10	5
1802, perfect dies	1 00	5	2
1803, small date: $\frac{1}{100}$ over $\frac{1}{000}$	2 00	25	5
1803, small date: small $\frac{1}{100}$	1 00	5	2
1803, small date: small $\frac{1}{100}$: stemless wreath	1 00	10	2
1803, small date: large $\frac{1}{100}$	1 00	5	2

	Uncirculated.	Fine.	Good.
1803, large date: small $\frac{1}{100}$: perfect 1	$1 00	$0 05	$0 02
1803, large date: large $\frac{1}{100}$: perfect 1	1 50	10	5
1804	25 00	5 00	1 00

NOTE: There are numerous counterfeits and re-strikes of this date.

1805, blunt 1	$5 00	$0 50	$0 05
1805, perfect 1	3 00	25	2
1806	5 00	50	5
1807, over 1806: perfect 1	3 00	25	2
1807, over 1806: blunt 1	4 00	30	5
1807, small $\frac{1}{100}$	2 00	25	2
1807, large $\frac{1}{100}$	3 00	20	5

Profile of Liberty l., with inscribed fillet. ℞ circular olive wreath.

1808	$5 00	$0 50	$0 05
1809, over 1808 (always)	10 00	1 00	25
1810, over 1809	3 00	25	2
1810, perfect date	2 00	10	2

This cut illustrates admirably the so-called *overstrikes*, which means that the dies used for the issues of 1810 were also used for the 1811, by simply changing the last figure. Some of these overstrikes are very rare and command higher prices than those with perfect dates. For instance, the half dollars of 1805 struck from the altered die of 1804 are very rare, also the cents of 1799 struck from the altered die of 1789, and so with a great many other overstrikes.

	Uncirculated.	Fine.	Good.
1811, over 1810	$3 00	$0 25	$0 02
1811, perfect date	2 00	10	2
1812, large date	2 00	5	2
1812, small date	3 00	10	5
1813	4 00	10	5
1814, crosslet 4	2 00	5	2
1814, plain 4	2 00	5	2

Profile of Liberty l., with inscribed coronet. ℞ like preceding.

1816	$0 50	$0 02	$0 01
1817, thirteen stars: wide date	50	2	1
1817, thirteen stars: compact date,	50	2	1
1817, thirteen stars: divided date,	50	2	1
1817, fifteen stars	1 00	10	2

	Uncirculated.	Fine.	Good.
1818, wide date	$0 50	$0 02	$0 01
1818, compact date	75	5	1
1819, over 1818: large date (always)	50	2	1
1819, small date: stars distant	40	2	1
1819, small, compact date: stars close	50	5	1
1820, over 1819: large date	40	2	1
1820, over 1819: small date	40	2	1
1820, small, perfect date	40	2	1
1820, large date	25	2	1
1821, wide date	2 00	50	5
1821, compact date	3 00	75	10
1822, wide date	2 00	5	1
1822, compact date	2 00	5	1
1823, over 1822	3 00	25	2
1823, perfect date	4 00	25	2
1824, over 1822	3 00	25	2
1824, wide date	2 00	15	1
1824, compact date	2 00	10	1
1825, large letters on R	3 00	25	2
1825, small letters on R	4 00	30	5
1826, over 1825	3 00	15	2
1826, wide date	2 00	10	1
1826, compact date	2 00	10	1
1827	2 00	10	1
1828, large date	2 00	10	1
1828, large date: outlined 8 beneath 2	3 00	15	2
1828, small date	3 00	15	2
1829, large letters on R	2 00	5	1
1829, small letters on R	2 00	5	1
1830, small letters on R	1 00	3	1
1830, large letters on R	1 00	2	1
1831, large letters on R	1 00	2	1
1831, small letters on R	1 00	2	1
1832, small letters on R	2 00	5	1
1832, small letters on R: ONE CENT large	3 00	5	1
1832, large letters on R	2 00	3	1
1833, large letters on R	2 00	3	1
1833, small letters on R	1 00	3	1
1834, small date and letters: large stars	1 00	3	1
1834, large date and letters: large stars	1 00	3	1

	Uncirculated.	Fine.	Good.
1834, large date: small letters and stars	$1 00	$0 03	$0 01
1835, large date and stars	1 00	3	1
1835, small date and stars	1 00	3	1
1835, small date and stars: newly engraved head (type 1836)	1 00	3	1
1836	1 00	3	1
1836, profile like 1835. R large letters	2 00	5	1
1837, plain cord in hair: large letters	1 00	2	1
1837, plain cord in hair: small letters	1 00	2	1
1837, beaded cord in hair: small letters	1 00	2	1
1838	1 00	2	1
1839, over 1836	2 00	5	1
1839, type of 1838	1 00	2	1

1839, "Silly" head: newly engraved dies	$1 00	$0 02	$0 01

	Uncirculated.	Fine.	Good.
1839, "Booby" head: newly engraved: no dash below CENT hereafter	$1 00	$0 02	$0 01

	Uncirculated.	Fine.	Good.
1839, type of 1840: newly engraved	$1 00	$0 02	$0 01
1840, large date	1 00	2	1
1840, large date: connected figures	1 00	2	1
1840, small date	1 00	2	1
1840, small date: double outlines to 18	1 00	2	1
1841	1 00	2	1
1842, small date	2 00	5	2
1842, large date	1 00	2	1
1843, type of 1842	1 00	2	1
1843, obv. like 1842. ℞ large letters (type 1844)	1 00	2	1
1843, head upright over date. ℞ large letters (type 1844)	1 00	2	1
1844, defective date (over other figures)	1 00	2	1
1844, perfect date	1 00	2	1
1845	1 00	2	1
1846, short figures	1 00	2	1
1846, short, double figures	1 00	2	1
1846, broad figures	1 00	2	1
1846, tall figures	1 00	2	1
1846, tall figures: crosslet 4 (one) 1847	1 00	2	1
1847, twice engraved date	1 00	2	1
1848, small date	2 00	10	5

	Uncirculated.	Fine.	Good.
1848, large date	$1 00	$0 02	$0 01
1848, large date, outlined figures,	50	2	1
1848, large date over other figures,	1 00	5	2
1849	1 00	5	1
1850	10	1	1
1850, connected 5	15	1	1
1851, over 1881!	25	1	1
1851	15	1	1
1852	15	1	1
1852, outlined figures	25	1	1
1853, outlined figures	25	1	1
1853	10	1	1
1854	15	1	1
1855, slanting 5's	10	1	1
1855, slanting 5's: flaw over ear	20	1	1
1855, upright 5's	5	1	1
1856, upright 5's	10	1	1
1856, slanting 5's	5	1	1
1857, large date	10	2	1
1857, small date	10	2	1

Cents, Nickel.

Authorized, act of February 21, 1857. Weight, 72 grains. Regular coinage commenced in 1857. Few were issued in 1856. Coinage discontinued in 1864.

Flying eagle to left. R value in cotton, tobacco and grain wreath.

	Proof.	Uncirculated.	Fine.
1856, copper-nickel	$3 00	$2 00	$1 00
1856, pure copper	3 50	2 00	1 00
1856, pure nickel	3 50	2 00	1 00

	Proof.	Uncirculated.	Fine.
1857, copper-nickel................	$0 10	$0 01	$0 01
1858, copper-nickel: large letters,	10	1	1
1858, copper-nickel: small letters,	10	1	1
1858, pure copper: small letters..	1 00	25	5

Profile of Liberty l., with feathered head-dress. ℞ value in olive wreath.

	Proof.	Uncirculated.	Fine.
1858, copper-nickel..............	15	1	1
1858, copper....................	25	5	2
1859, copper-nickel..............	5	1	1
1859, copper....................	25	5	2

Same obv. ℞ value beneath shield in oak wreath.

	Proof.	Uncirculated.	Fine.
1859, copper-nickel..............	10	1	1
1860, copper-nickel..............	5	1	1
1861, copper-nickel..............	5	1	1
1862, copper-nickel..............	2	1	1
1863, copper-nickel..............	3	1	1
1863, copper-nickel: milled edge,	10	1	1
1863, bronze....................	10	1	1
1864, copper-nickel..............	5	1	1
1864, bronze....................	5	1	1
1864, oreide....................	25	1	1

Cent, Bronze.

Authorized, act of April 22, 1864. Weight 48 grains. Regular coinage commenced in 1864.

	Proof.	Uncirculated.
1864, bronze, L (Longacre) on ribbon (and on all following).............	$0 10	$0 01
1865, copper-nickel................	50	1

	Proof.	Uncirculated.
1865, pure nickel	$0 50	$0 01
1865, bronze	10	1
1866	10	1
1867	5	1
1868	5	1
1869	5	1
1870	5	1
1871	5	1
1872	5	1
1873	5	1
1874	3	1
1875	3	1
1876	3	1
1877	3	1
1877, pure nickel	1 00	10
1878	3	1
1879	3	1
1880	3	1
1881	3	1
1881, pure nickel	1 00	10
1882	3	1
1883	3	1
1884	3	1
1885	3	1
1886	3	1
1887	3	1
1888	3	1
1889	3	1
1890	3	1

Half Cent.

Authorized, act April 2, 1792. Weight, 132 grains. Weight changed, act of January 14, 1793, to 104 grains, and act of March 3, 1795, to 84 grains. Coinage commenced in 1793, and discontinued in 1857.

	Uncirculated.	Fine.	Good.
Profile of Liberty l., with cap on pole. ℞ value in laurel wreath.			
1793, lettered edge: small date	$10 00	$2 00	$1 00
1793, lettered edge: large date	12 00	2 00	1 00

	Uncirculated.	Fine.	Good.
Profile of Liberty r., cap on pole. ℞ value in olive wreath.			
1794, lettered edge	$3 00	$0 50	$0 10
1795, lettered edge	3 00	50	10
1795, lettered edge: punctuated date, 1,795	5 00	75	25
1795, plain edge: punctuated date, 1,795	2 00	50	10
1795, plain edge: *without* pole	3 00	75	10
1796, plain edge: *without* pole	50 00	25 00	5 00
1796, plain edge: with pole	60 00	30 00	6 00
1797, lettered edge: with pole: large date	10 00	2 00	1 00
1797, plain edge: with pole: large date	2 00	50	10
1797, 1 over date: with pole: large date	2 00	50	10
1797, small date: with pole	3 00	75	25
Draped bust of Liberty r. ℞ similar to preceding.			
1800	1 00	25	5
1802, over 1800 (always)	5 00	75	25
1803, over 1802	50	5	2
1803, perfect date	25	2	1
1804, plain 4	50	10	5
1804, plain 4: stemless wreath	25	2	1
1804, crosslet 4: stemless wreath	50	10	5

	Uncirculated.	Fine.	Good.
1804, crosslet 4	$ 25	$0 02	$0 01
1804, crosslet 4: protruding tongue and chin	30	5	2
1805, over 1803	35	10	5
1805, stemless wreath	30	5	2
1806, stemless wreath: small 6	25	5	2
1806, large 6	25	5	2
1807	30	5	2
1808, over 1807	50	10	5
1808, perfect date	25	5	2

Profile of Liberty l., with inscribed fillet. ℞ circular olive wreath.

	Uncirculated.	Fine.	Good.
1809, over 1806! (9 first sunk inverted)	$0 25	$0 05	$0 02
1809, inner circle to o in date	25	5	2
1809, perfect date	20	5	2
1810,	25	5	2
1811,	2 00	50	15
1825	10	5	2
1826	10	5	2
1828, twelve stars	15	6	2
1828, thirteen stars	10	5	2
1829	15	6	2
1831, proofs only	10 00	3 00	1 00
1831, re-strike with ℞ of 1856: proof $4.00	3 00	1 00	50
1832	10	5	2
1833	10	5	2
1834	10	5	2
1835	10	5	2
1836, proofs only	10 00	3 00	1 00
1836, re-strike with ℞ of 1856: proof $4.00	3 00	1 00	50

	Proof, Originals.	Proof, Re-strikes.	Uncirculated.
Profile of Liberty l., with inscribed coronet. ℞ similar to preceding, without dash.			
1840, re-strikes have small berries: originals *large* berries........	$10 00	$3 00	$1 00
1841, re-strikes have small berries: originals *large* berries........	10 00	3 00	1 00
1842, re-strikes have small berries: originals *large* berries........	10 00	3 00	1 00
1843, re-strikes have small berries: originals *large* berries........	10 00	3 00	1 00
1844, re-strikes have small berries: originals *large* berries........	10 00	3 00	1 00
1845, re-strikes have small berries: originals *large* berries........	10 00	3 00	1 00
1846, re-strikes have small berries: originals *large* berries........	10 00	3 00	1 00
1847, re-strikes have small berries: originals *large* berries........	10 00	3 00	1 00
1848, re-strikes have small berries: originals *large* berries........	10 00	3 00	1 00
1849, small date.................	15		5
1849, large date.................	15		5
1850............................	10		5
1851............................	10		5
1852............................	5 00		2 00
1853............................	10		5
1854............................	10		5
1854, copper nickel.............	10 00		3 00
1855............................	10		5
1856............................	10		5
1857, coinage discontinued......	10		5

Jackson Cent, or Hard Times Token.

Coined 1834 to 1841. There are over 100 various designs, all about the size of the large copper cent, and they are worth from 2 cents to $2.00 None are very rare.

	Uncirculated.	Fine.	Good.
Andrew Jackson	$2 00	$1 00	$0 25

Perish credit, perish commerce: boar running	$0 25	$0 05	$0 02

Executive sub-treasury: tortoise carrying safe	$0 25	$0 05	$0 02

Van Buren: ship, falling masts	$0 50	$0 25	$0 10

	Uncirculated.	Fine.	Good.
Webster: ship sailing...........	$0 25	$0 10	$0 05

Confederate States.

These tokens, intended for circulation in the south, were struck a few months prior to the civil war as a speculative venture. In attempting to move them south shortly after the breaking out of the war, they were confiscated by the Federal government.

	Uncirculated.	Fine.	Good.
1861, half dollar: shield and Liberty cap. CONFEDERATE STATES OF AMERICA. ℞ same as obv. of U. S. Half Dollar...	$50 00	$25 00	$5 00
1860, token: palmetto tree: NO SUBMISSION TO THE NORTH. ℞ tobacco plant: THE WEALTH OF THE SOUTH, etc: (4 var.): brass........................	1 00	25	10
Token without date: shield: OUR RIGHTS THE CONSTITUTION AND THE UNION. ℞ as last...	1 00	30	15

War Tokens.

Issued by different parties during the late war of the Rebellion. There are about 500 different patterns. None are very valuable, and average not over 5 cents apiece. I have no use for them and do not buy them at present.

Postage Stamps.

Enclosed in metal cases, and used as currency 1863-64.

			Fine.
1 Cent.	Blue		$0 05
3 "	Red		5
5 "	Brown		10
10 "	Green		20
12 "	Black		25
24 "	Violet		25
30 "	Orange		50
90 "	Blue		1 00

Silver Dollar.

For prices paid see quotations of silver dollars.

These Cuts were left out from the regular quotations by mistake.

New York State Cent. *Excelsior.* For prizes paid see New York coins.

This coin is of unknown origin, and found only engraved. Will pay for good specimen, $10.00.

Washington Cent. Liverpool.

Statement of Coinage from the Organization of the Mint—1793 to 1882.

GOLD COINAGE.

Period.	Double Eagles.	Eagles.	Half Eagles.	Three Dollars.	Quarter Eagles.	Dollars.
1793 to 1795		$27,950	$43,535			
1796		69,340	30,980		$2,407.50	
1797		83,230	18,045		2,147.50	
1798		79,740	124,335		1,535.00	
1799		174,830	37,255		1,200.00	
1800		259,650	58,110			
1801		292,540	130,030			
1802		150,900	265,880		6,530.00	
1803		89,790	167,530		1,057.50	
1804		97,950	152,375		8,317.50	
1805			165,915		4,452.50	
1806			320,465		4,040.00	
1807			420,465		17,030.00	
1808			277,890		6,775.00	
1809			169,375			
1810			501,435			
1811			497,905			
1812			290,435			

Year			
1813	477,140		
1814	77,270		
1815	3,175		
1816			
1817			
1818			
1819	242,940		
1820	258,615		
1821	1,319,030	16,120.00	
1822	173,205		
1823	88,980		
1824	72,425	6,500.00	
1825	86,700	11,085.00	
1826	145,300	1,900.00	
1827	90,345	7,000.00	
1828	124,565		
1829	140,145	8,507.50	
1830	287,210	11,350.00	
1831	631,755	11,300.00	
1832	702,970	11,000.00	
1833	787,435	10,400.00	
1834	968,150	293,425.00	
1835	3,660,845	328,505.00	
1836	1,857,670	1,369,965.00	
1837	2,765,735	112,700.00	
1838	1,035,605	137,310.00	72,000
1839	1,600,285	170,660.00	382,480
	802,745		

Statement of Coinage From the Organization of the Mint—1793 to 1882.—Continued.

GOLD COINAGE.

Period.	Double Eagles.	Eagles.	Half Eagles.	Three Dollars.	Quarter Eagles.	Dollars.
1840	....	$473,380	$1,048,360	....	$153,562.50	....
1841	....	656,310	380,725	....	54,562.50	....
1842	....	1,089,070	655,330	....	89,770.00	....
1843	....	2,506,240	4,275,425	....	1,327,132.50	....
1844	....	1,250,610	4,088,275	....	89,345.00	....
1845	....	736,530	2,743,640	....	276,277.50	....
1846	....	1,018,750	2,736,155	....	279,272.50	....
1847	....	14,337,640	5,401,685	....	482,060.00	....
1848	....	1,813,340	1,863,560	....	98,612.50	....
1849	....	6,775,180	1,184,645	....	111,147.50	$936,789
1850	$26,225,220	3,489,510	860,160	....	895,547.50	511,301
1851	48,043,100	4,393,280	2,651,955	....	3,867,337.50	3,658,820
1852	44,860,520	2,311,060	3,689,635	....	3,283,827.50	2,201,145
1853	26,646,520	2,522,530	2,305,095	....	3,519,615.00	4,384,149
1854	18,052,340	2,305,760	1,513,195	$491,214	1,896,397.50	1,657,012
1855	24,636,820	1,487,010	1,257,090	171,465	600,700.00	824,833
1856	30,277,560	1,484,900	1,751,655	181,530	1,213,117.50	1,788,996
1857	14,056,300	129,160	673,610	38,496	320,465.00	593,532

1858	28,038,880	629,900	772,775	66,177	515,632.50	230,361
1859	16,236,720	146,000	406,710	34,572	213,010.00	259,065
1860	15,458,800	342,130	361,145	61,206	128,980.00	93,215
1861	59,316,420	552,050	452,590	18,216	338,440.00	15,521
1862	36,247,500	972,990	3,287,160	17,355	3,208,122.50	1,799,259
1863	20,387,720	126,580	117,010	117	62,475.00	1,950
1864	21,465,640	85,800	51,500	16,470	23,185.00	6,750
1865	24,879,600	93,750	86,075	10,065	30,502.50	7,225
1866	27,494,900	376,100	300,750	12,090	122,975.00	7,130
1867	27,925,400	51,150	154,475	7,875	73,062.50	5,225
1868	17,705,800	155,500	153,750	14,700	74,125.00	10,550
1869	21,270,500	209,350	228,925	7,575	105,862.50	5,925
1870	22,018,480	89,130	94,625	10,605	35,137.50	9,335
1871	20,919,240	163,250	158,625	4,020	53,400.00	3,940
1872	19,798,500	254,600	243,700	6,090	72,575.00	1,030
1873	34,765,500	204,650	237,525	75	39,062.50	2,525
1874	48,283,900	383,480	809,780	125,460	516,150.00	323,920
1875	32,748,140	599,840	203,655	60	2,250.00	20
1876	37,896,720	153,610	71,800	135	53,052.50	3,645
1877	43,941,700	56,200	67,835	4,464	5,780.00	2,220
1878	51,406,340	155,490	688,680	137,850	408,900.00	1,720
1879	37,234,340	1,031,440	1,442,130	109,182	1,166,800.00	3,020
1880	21,515,360	18,836,320	15,790,860	9,090	3,075.00	3,030
1881	15,345,520	33,389,050	29,982,180	4,698	9,140.00	3,276
1882	14,563,920	44,369,410	30,473,955	75	62.50	6,025
Total	$949,663,920	$153,488,930	$147,790,620	$1,560,927	$28,383,727.50	$19,362,509

Statement of Coinage from the Organization of the Mint—1793 to 1882.

SILVER COINAGE.

Period.	Trade Dollars.	Dollars.	Half Dollars.	Quarter Dollars.	Twenty Cents.	Dimes.
1793 to 1795		$204,791				
1796		72,920	$161,572.00			
1797		7,776	1,959.00	$1,473.50		$2,213.50
1798		327,536		63.00		2,526.10
1799		423,515				2,755.00
1800		220,920				
1801		54,454	15,144.50			2,176.00
1802		41,650	14,945.00			3,464.00
1803		66,064	15,857.50			1,097.50
1804		19,570	73,259.50	1,684.50		3,304.00
1805		321	105,861.00	30,348.50		826.50
1806			419,788.00	51,531.00		12,078.00
1807			525,788.00	55,160.75		16,500.00
1808			684,300.00			
1809			702,905.00			4,471.00
1810			638,138.00			635.50
1811			601,822.00			
1812			814,029.50			6,518.00

125

Year				
1813		620,951.50		
1814		519,537.50		42,150
1815				
1816		23,575.00	17,308.00	
1817		607,783.50	5,000.75	
1818		980,161.00		
1819		1,104,002.00	90,293.50	
1820		375,561.00	36,000.00	94,258.70
1821		652,898.50	31,861.00	118,651.20
1822		779,786.50	54,212.75	10,000.00
1823		847,100.00	16,020.00	44,000.00
1824		1,752,477.00	4,450.00	
1825		1,471,583.00		51,000.00
1826		2,002,090.00	42,000.00	
1827		2,746,700.00		121,500.00
1828		1,537,600.00	1,000.00	12,500.00
1829		1,856,078.00	25,500.00	77,000.00
1830		2,382,400.00		51,000.00
1831		2,936,830.00	99,500.00	77,135.00
1832		2,398,500.00	80,000.00	52,250.00
1833		2,603,000.00	39,000.00	48,500.00
1834		3,206,002.00	71,500.00	63,500.00
1835		2,676,003.00	488,000.00	141,000.00
1836	1,000	3,273,100.00	118,000.00	119,000.00
1837		1,814,910.00	63,100.00	104,200.00
1838		1,773,000.00	208,000.00	239,493.00
1839	300	1,717,280.50	122,786.50	229,471.50

Statement of Coinage from the Organization of the Mint—1793 to 1882.—Continued.

SILVER COINAGE.

Period.	Trade Dollars.	Dollars.	Half Dollars.	Quarter Dollars.	Twenty Cents.	Dimes.
1840	.....	$61,005	$1,145,054.00	$153,331.75	.....	$253,358.00
1841	.....	173,000	355,500.00	143,000.00	.....	363,000.00
1842	.....	184,618	1,484,882.00	214,250.00	.....	390,750.00
1843	.....	165,100	3,056,000.00	403,400.00	.....	152,000.00
1844	.....	20,000	1,885,500.00	290,300.00	.....	7,250.00
1845	.....	24,500	1,341,500.00	230,500.00	.....	198,500.00
1846	.....	169,600	2,257,000.00	127,500.00	.....	3,130.00
1847	.....	140,750	1,870,000.00	280,500.00	.....	24,500.00
1848	.....	15,000	1,880,000.00	36,500.00	.....	45,150.00
1849	.....	62,600	1,781,000.00	85,000.00	.....	113,900.00
1850	.....	47,500	1,341,500.00	150,700.00	.....	244,150.00
1851	.....	1,300	301,375.00	62,000.00	.....	142,650.00
1852	.....	1,100	110,565.00	68,265.00	.....	196,550.00
1853	.....	46,110	2,439,354.00	4,146,555.00	.....	1,327,301.00
1854	.....	33,140	4,111,000.00	3,466,000.00	.....	624,000.00
1855	.....	26,000	2,284,725.00	861,350.00	.....	207,500.00
1856	.....	63,500	1,903,500.00	2,129,500.00	.....	696,000.00
1857	.....	94,000	114,000.00	583,000.00	.....	489,000.00

Year						Total
1858						226,000.00
1859			288,500	4,430,000.00		229,000.00
1860			600,530	4,005,500.00		98,600.00
1861			559,900	1,627,400.00		167,300.00
1862			1,750	959,650.00		158,405.00
1863			31,400	1,785,425.00		34,071.00
1864			23,170	983,630.00		14,037.00
1865			32,900	483,985.00		17,160.00
1866			58,550	553,100.00		21,065.00
1867			57,000	579,525.00		13,670.00
1868			54,800	897,450.00		73,315.00
1869			231,350	946,750.00		23,905.00
1870			588,308	561,675.00		98,185.00
1871			657,929	1,009,375.00		10,707.50
1872			1,112,961	1,242,771.00		222,471.50
1873			977,150	1,486,492.50		419,040.00
1874	$3,588,900			1,199,775.00		497,255.80
1875	5,697,500			1,438,930.00		889,560.00
1876	6,132,050			2,853,500.00	$5,858.00	3,639,105.00
1877	9,162,900			4,985,525.00	263,500.00	2,055,070.00
1878	11,378,010			9,746,350.00	1,440.00	760,891.00
1879			8,573,500	3,875,255.00	142.00	45.00
1880			27,227,500	225.00		1,575.00
1881			27,933,750	3,275.00		3,695.50
1882			27,637,955	4,677.50		2,507.50
			27,772,075	5,537.50		
Total	$35,959,360		$127,190,618	$122,758,510.50	$271,000.00	$16,910,500.30
				$38,487,997.50		

Statement of Coinage from the Organization of the Mint—1793 to 1882.—Continued.

Period.	SILVER COINAGE.			MINOR COINAGE.			
	Half Dimes.	Three Cents.	Five Cents.	Three Cents.	Two Cents.	Cents.	Half Cents.
1793–1795	$4,320.80	....	....	....	....	$10,660.33	$712.67
1796	511.50	....	....	....	....	9,747.00	577.40
1797	2,226.35	....	....	....	....	8,975.10	535.24
1798	....	....	....	....	....	9,797.00	....
1799	....	....	....	....	....	9,045.85	60.83
1800	1,200.00	....	....	....	....	28,221.75	1,057.65
1801	1,695.50	....	....	....	....	13,628.37	....
1802	650.50	....	....	....	....	34,351.00	71.83
1803	1,892.50	....	....	....	....	24,713.53	489.50
1804	....	....	....	....	....	7,568.38	5,276.56
1805	....	....	....	....	....	9,411.16	4,072.32
1806	780.00	....	....	....	....	3,480.00	1,780.00
1807	....	....	....	....	....	7,272.21	2,380.00
1808	....	....	....	....	....	11,090.00	2,000.00
1809	....	....	....	....	....	2,228.67	5,772.86
1810	....	....	....	....	....	14,585.00	1,075.00
1811	....	....	....	....	....	2,180.25	315.70
1812	....	....	....	....	....	10,755.00	....

1813			4,180.00
1814			3,578.30
1815			
1816			28,209.82
1817			39,484.00
1818			31,670.00
1819			26,710.00
1820			44,075.50
1821			3,890.00
1822			20,723.39
1823			
1824			12,620.00
1825		315.00	14,611.00
1826		1,170.00	15,174.25
1827			23,577.32
1828		3,030.00	22,606.24
1829	61,500.00	2,435.00	14,145.00
1830	62,000.00		17,115.00
1831	62,135.00	11.00	33,592.60
1832	48,250.00		23,620.00
1833	68,500.00	770.00	27,390.00
1834	74,000.00	600.00	18,551.00
1835	138,000.00	705.00	38,784.00
1836	95,000.00		21,110.00
1837	113,800.00	1,990.00	55,583.00
1838	112,750.00		63,702.00
1839	106,457.50		31,286.61

Statement of Coinage from the Organization of the Mint—1793 to 1882—Continued.

	SILVER COINAGE.		MINOR COINAGE.				
Period.	Half Dimes.	Three Cents.	Five Cents.	Three Cents.	Two Cents.	Cents.	Half Cents.
1840	$113,954.25					$24,627.00	
1841	98,250.00					15,973.67	
1842	58,250.00					23,833.90	
1843	58,250.00					24,283.20	
1844	32,500.00					23,987.52	
1845	78,200.00					38,948.04	
1846	1,350.00					41,208.00	
1847	63,700.00					61,836.69	
1848	63,400.00					64,157.99	
1849	72,450.00					41,785.00	$199.32
1850	82,250.00					44,268.44	199.06
1851	82,050.00	$185,022.00				98,897.07	738.36
1852	63,025.00	559,905.00				50,630.94	
1853	785,251.00	342,000.00				66,411.31	648.47
1854	365,000.00	20,130.00				42,361.56	276.79
1855	117,500.00	4,170.00				15,748.29	282.50
1856	299,000.00	43,740.00				26,904.63	202.15
1857	197,000.00					63,334.56	175.90

	1	2	3	4	5	6	7
1858	327,000.00					234,000.00	
1859	195,000.00					307,000.00	
1860	96,500.00					342,000.00	
1861	139,350.00	37,980.00				101,660.00	
1862	117,627.50	41,400.00				116,000.00	
1863	8,223.00	16,440.00				478,450.00	
1864	4,518.50	7,950.00		$36,450		427,350.00	
1865	4,880.00	18,256.50		535,600		541,800.00	
1866	10,732.50	2,803.80	$105,930.00	122,980		187,080.00	
1867	435.00	11.10	270,270.00	69,880	$66,240.00	113,750.00	
1868	24,290.00	618.00	133,410.00	61,330	1,562,500.00	98,565.00	
1869		679.50	108,390.00	34,615	1,445,100.00	78,810.00	
1870	527.50	141.00	64,380.00	22,890	1,101,250.00	58,365.00	
1871	48,222.50	120.00	42,600.00	22,105	487,500.00	62,075.00	
1872	14,396.25	151.50	27,630.00	6,170	171,950.00	9,320.00	
1873	152,751.75	115.50	18,330.00		89,200.00	107,330.00	
1874	175,442.50	129.75	34,320.00		352,400.00	137,935.00	
1875		61.05	29,640.00	?	244,350.00	123,185.00	
1876		25.50	12,540.60		94,650.00	120,090.00	
1877			7,500.00		132,700.00	36,915.00	
1878					25,250.00	30,566.00	
1879			48.00		80.00	95,639.00	
1880			984.00		1,175.00	267,741.50	
1881			982.50		1,247.50	372,513.55	
1882			32,416.65		177.75	42,644.75	
			104.25		220,038.75		
Total	$4,906,946.90	$1,281,850.20	$5,995,809.00	$889,625.40	$912,020	$6,495,654.24	$39,926.11

U. S. Fractional Currency.

First General Issue, Aug. 21, 1862, to May 27, 1863.

Postal Currency; Act of July 17, 1862.

		Price with A. B. Co.	Price without A. B. Co.
No. 1.—	5 Cents; bust Jefferson, brown, perforated edges	20 cts.	30 cts.
" 2.—	10 Cents; bust Washington, green, perforated edges	20 "	40 "
" 3.—	25 Cents; 5 busts Jefferson, brown, perforated edges	75 "	90 "
" 4.—	50 Cents; 5 busts Washington, green, perforated edges	80 "	$1 20
" 5.—	5 Cents; like No. 1, but unperf'd.	7 "	20 "
" 6.—	10 " " No. 2, " "	15 "	20 "
" 7.—	25 " " No. 3, " "	30 "	40 "
" 8.—	50 " " No. 4, " "	60 "	80 "

Second General Issue, Oct. 10, 1863, to Feb. 23, 1863.

These, and all following, issued under Act of March 3, 1863.

		Plain Paper.	Fibre Paper.
No. 9.—	5 Cents; bust Washington in bronze frame; rev. brown	7 cts.	
" 10.—	10 Cents; bust Washington in bronze frame; rev. green	15 "	
" 11.—	25 Cents; bust Washington in bronze frame; rev. purple	30 "	
" 12.—	50 Cents; bust Washington in bronze frame; rev. rose	—	"
" 13.—	5 Cents; like No. 9, with bronze letter and figures on rev.	15 "	25 cts.
" 14.—	10 Cents; like No. 10, with bronze letter and figures on rev.	15 "	30 "
" 15.—	25 Cents; like No. 11, with bronze letter and figures on rev.	40 "	60 "
" 16.—	50 Cents; like No. 12, with bronze letter and figures on reverse, vermilion	70 "	80 "

Third General Issue, Dec. 5, to Aug. 16, 1869.

All following have green backs, exceptions noted; some with bronze numerals and letters on reverse.

	Plain Paper.	Fibre Paper.
No. 17.— 3 Cents; bust Washington, dark curtain	25 cts.	
" 18.— 3 Cents; different bust Washington, light curtain	10 "	
" 19.— 5 Cents; bust Clark	10 "	
" 20.—10 " " Washington	15 "	
" 21.—25 " " Fessenden, white "25" in solid bronze field		$5 00
" 22.—25 Cents; bust Fessenden, outline "25" in open ornamental frame	30 "	1 30
" 23.—50 Cents; figure Justice	50 "	1 00
" 24.—50 " bust Spinner, rev. like preceding	60 "	1 00
" 25.—50 Cents; bust Spinner, rev. large "50" in centre	75 "	

Second Series of Third Issue.

Carmine backs.

	Autos. Colby & Spinner.	Autos. Jeffries & Spinner.
No. 26.— 5 Cents, like No. 19, printed signatures.. 25 cts.		
" 27.—10 Cents; like No. 20, printed signatures.. 40 "	60 cts.	1 00
" 28.—25 Cents; like No. 22, printed signatures.. 70 "		
" 29.—50 Cents; like No. 23, printed signatures.. 80 "	1 00	
" 30.—50 Cents; like No. 24, printed signatures.. 80 "	1 00	

Proof impressions (obverses and reverses separate) of the first three issues, generally printed on paper watermarked "C S A" (captured from the English blockade runners, bound for the Confederacy), furnished at lowest prices.

FOURTH GENERAL ISSUE, JULY 14, 1869, TO FEB. 16, 1875.

	Minute red fibre.	Coarse red fibre.	Blue r. ends violet fibre large and small seals.
No. 31.—10 Cents; bust Liberty large seal............	10 cts.	10 cts.	10 cts.
" 32.—15 Cents; bust Pallas, large seal............	25 "	20 "	20 "
" 33.—25 Cents; bust Washington, large seal.......	25 "	25 "	25 "
" 34.—50 Cents; bust Lincoln, large seal............	80 "	60 "	
" 35.—50 Cents; bust Stanton, large seal............			75 "

SECOND SERIES OF FOURTH ISSUE.

	Violet fibre.
No. 36.—10 Cents; bust Meredith, green seal, A-1 to N-72............................	15 cts.
" 37.—50 Cents; bust Dexter, green seal, A-1 to N-72............................	75 "

FIFTH GENERAL ISSUE, FEB. 26, 1874, TO FEB. 15, 1876.

	Long key in seal.	Short key in seal.
No. 38.—10 Cents; bust Meredith, red seal, A-1 to N-72...	10 cts.	10 cts.
" 39.—25 Cents; bust Walker, red seal, A-1 to N-72................	25 "	25 "
" 40.—50 Cents; bust Crawford, red seal, A-1 to N-72................	50 "	50 "

ESSAYS FOR 15-CENT NOTE.

Obv. and Rev. always separate.

A—Busts of Grant and Sherman; rev. green or red, printed signatures.........................	$2 00
B—Busts of Grant and Sherman; rev. green or red, autos. of Jeffries and Spinner...............	2 25
C—Busts of Grant and Sherman; rev. green or red, autos. of Allison and Spinner...............	2 25

LIST OF
Counterfeit U. S. Treasury and Nat'l Bank Notes.

IMPORTANT EXPLANATION TO THE TRADE.—The Government prints all the Paper Money in the country, both Greenbacks and National Bank Notes, on sheets of four bills each, lettered A B C D; some one of these letters is on every bill, and is a fixture on the plates. The counterfeiter makes his plate invariably a single one from some one bill, and never prints but one of the four letters. This leaves the other three letters on the same bank undisturbed, and as every effort to substitute another letter on the National notes has failed, the other three letters of these notes can be taken with impunity; but the letter counterfeited on all notes must be refused by non-experts, as the Redemption Agency retires all the genuine of that letter and thus leaves the field to the counterfeit. This principle is so explicit and comprehensible that without ever seeing a bill, if the letter and denomination be given, its quality can be positively ascertained.

Counterfeit National Bank Notes.

* Banks marked with an * do not exist, and the whole issue is fraudulent.

1s.

Boston, Mass............................National Eagle..................Photo Letter A, July 1, 1865.

2s.

Kinderhook, N. Y.	National Union	Letter A,	July 1, 1865.
*Linderpark, N. Y.	National Union	" A,	July 1, 1865.
Newport, R. I.	National Bank of Rhode Island	" A,	Nov.[1, 1865.
New York, N. Y.	Ninth	" A,	Jan. 2, 1865.
" " "	Marine	" A,	July 1, 1865.
" " "	Market	" A,	July 1, 1865.
" " "	St. Nicholas	" A,	July 1, 1865.
Peekskill, N. Y.	Westchester County	" A,	Aug. 15, 1865.

5s.

Amsterdam, N. Y.	Manufacturers'	Letter B,	April 15, 1875.
Aurora, Ill.	First	" A,	Nov. 2, 1863.
Boston, Mass.	Globe .... Photo	" C,	
"	Pacific .... Photo	" B,	Series 1875.
"	Boylston National ... Photo	" C,	Series 1875.
Battle Creek, Mich.	First National	" B,	June 10, 1876.
Canton, Ill.	First	" A,	May 21, 1805.
Castleton, N. Y.	National Bank of Castleton	" D,	March 10, 1865.
*Cecil, Ill.	First	" A,	May 10, 1865.
Chicago, Ill.	First	" A,	May 10, 1805.
"	Central	" A,	May 10, 1865.
"	Merchants'	" A,	May 10, 1865.
"	Traders'	" A,	May 10, 1865.
"	German	" A,	March 10, 1865.
"	Union	" A,	March 10, 1865.
"	National Bank of Illinois	" A,	May 10, 1865.

Dedham, Mass.	Dedham	Photo	Letter B, Series 1875.
Fall River, Mass.	Pocasset	Photo	" C, Jan. 2, 1865.
*Galena, Ill.	First		" A, May 10, 1865.
Hanover, Pa.	First		" D, Feb. 20, 1864.
Jackson, Mich.	People's		" D, Oct. 2, 1865.
Jewitt City, Conn.	Jewitt City		" B, Sept. 1, 1865.
Johnsbury, Vt.	First National	Photo	" C, Aug. 6, 1864.
Leicester, Mass.	National Bank	Photo 333,764	" C, April 20, 1875.
Lockport, N.Y.	Niagara County National Bank		" C, Oct. 10, 1865.
Montpelier, Vt.	Montpelier	Photo	" A, Series 1875.
Milwaukee, Wis.	First National, No. A, 347,147		" B, Series 1882.
New Bedford, Mass.	Merchants'		" C, Feb. 14, 1865.
Northampton, Mass.	First		" C, May 2, 1864.
Paxton, Ill.	First		" A, Oct. 20, 1871.
Pawling, N.Y.	National Bank of Pawling		" A, July 20, 1865.
Peru, Ill.	First		" A, June 2, 1864.
Rome, N.Y.	Fort Stanwix		" B, Sept. 1, 1865.
Southbridge, Mass.	Southbridge	Photo	" B, May 10, 1875.
Tamaqua, Pa.	First		" B, July 1, 1865.
Troy, N.Y.	National State Bank		" A, May 10, 1865.
Virginia, Ill.	First National		" C,
Westfield, Mass.	Farmers'		" A, May 10, 1865.
	Hampden		" C and D, Aug. 1, 1865.

10s.

Albany, N.Y.	Albany City		Letter A, July 20, 1865.
Auburn, N.Y.	Auburn City		" A, July 20, 1865.
Buffalo, N.Y.	Farmers' and Manufacturers'		" A, Aug. 1, 1865.

Cincinnati, Ohio	Third National	Letter C, Series 1882.	
Lafayette, Ind.	Lafayette	" A, Dec. 22, 1874.	
Lockport, N. Y.	First	" A, Feb. 20, 1865.	
Muncie, Ind.	Muncie	" A, Feb. 14, 1865.	
Newburgh, N. Y.	Highland	" A, July 1, 1865.	
New York, N. Y.	American	" A, July 1, 1865.	
"	First, altered from American	" A, July 1, 1865.	
"	Marine	" A, July 1, 1865.	
"	Market	" A, July 1, 1865.	
"	Mechanics'	" A, July 1, 1865.	
"	National Bank of Commerce	" A, July 1, 1865.	
"	National Bank State of New York	" A, July 1, 1865.	
"	Union National Bank	" A, July 1, 1865.	
"	Croton National Bank	" A, July 1, 1865.	
"	Merchants' National Bank	" A, July 19, 1865.	
Philadelphia, Pa.	First	" B, Feb. 20, 1864.	
"	Third	" B, Feb. 20, 1864.	
Poughkeepsie, N. Y.	First	" A, July 5, 1865.	
"	City	" A, July 5, 1865.	
"	Farmers' and Manufacturers'	" A, Aug. 1, 1865.	
Red Hook, N. Y.	First	" A, Feb. 20, 1865.	
Richmond, Ind.	Richmond	" A, March 15, 1873.	
Rochester, N. Y.	Flour City	" A, July 1, 1865.	
Rome, N. Y.	Central	" A, May 12, 1865.	
Syracuse, N. Y.	Syracuse	" A, Aug. 1, 1865.	
Troy, N. Y.	Mutual	" A, May 10, 1865.	
Waterford, N. Y.	Saratoga County	" A, July ?, 1865.	
Watkins, N. Y.	Watkins	" A, Aug. 1, 1865.	

20s.

Indianapolis, Ind.	First	Letter A, Nov. 2, 1863.
New York, N. Y.	First	" B, July 19, 1865.
" " "	Market	" B, Jan. 19, 1865.
" " "	National Bank of Commerce	" B, Jan. 19, 1865.
" " "	Merchants'	" B, July 19, 1865.
" " "	National Shoe and Leather	" B, July 19, 1865.
†New York	Tradesmen's	" B, July 19, 1865.
Philadelphia, Pa.	Fourth	" A, March 7, 1864.
Portland, Conn.	First	" A, May 10, 1865.
*Utica, N. Y.	City	" B, Aug. 19, 1865.
Utica, N. Y.	Oneida	" B, Aug. 19, 1865.

50s.

Buffalo, N. Y.	Third	Letter A, March 10, 1865.
New York, N. Y.	Central	" A, April 15, 1864.
New York, N. Y.	Metropolitan	" A, Jan. 10, 1865.
New York, N. Y.	Mechanics'	" C, April 29, 1865.
*New York, N. Y.	Union	" A, April 15, 1865.
New York, N. Y.	National Broadway	" A & C, Jan. 10, 1865.
" " "	National Bank of Commerce	" A & C, Jan. 10, 1865.
" " "	Tradesmen's	" A & D, April 20, 1865.

100s.

Baltimore, Md.	National Exchange	Letter A, July 1, 1865.
Boston, Mass.	First	" A, Feb. 2, 1864.
" "	National Revere	" A, July 20, 1865.

† The date on this note is incomplete. It reads simply "U 19th, 1865."

Stolen National Bank Notes, with Forged Signatures.

The National Bank Notes described below were stolen when unsigned, the signature of the Bank Officers forged, and the Notes put in circulation. They are rejected when presented for redemption at the National Redemption Agency.

Name of Bank.	Denomination.	Bank Number.	Lower Left Corner.	Treasury Number.	Upper Right Corner.
First National Bank, Jersey City, N. J. ... 50s and 100s		671	750	19609	19669
Kansas City National Bank............ 10s		1198	2198	31826	32326
" " " 20s		711	7611	27172	27672
" " " 50s		697	1197	29266	29446
Merchants' National Bank, Albany, N. Y.... 10s and 20s		759	766	45195	45202
National Bank of Barre, Vt............ 10s and 20s		911	936	932805	932830
National Hide and Leather Bank, Boston ... 10s and 20s		11919	11972	22900	22925
National City Bank, Lynn, Mass.......... 50s and 100s		121	150	66796	66825
National Bank of Pontiac, Ill............ 5s		741	765	252111	252135
Osage National Bank, Osage, Iowa......... 5s		1751	2200	560958	561407
Third National Bank, New York......... 10s and 20s		9414	9428	644416	644430

Cincinnati, Ohio............Ohio..........Letter A, Dec. 22, 1864.
New York, N. Y.............Central......." A, April 15, 1864.
New Bedford, Mass..........Merchants'...." A, Feb. 14, 1865.
Pittsburgh, Pa..............National Bank of Commerce ...." A, Series 1875.
Pittsfield, Mass.............Pittsfield....." A, July 20, 1865.
Wilkesbarre, Pa.............Second........" A, Nov. 2, 1863.

Counterfeit Silver Certificates.

☞ *Examine all Silver Certificates with great care.*

1. *Of the denomination of* $10. Check-letter D, payable at Washington, D. C. No. 1650916, Series of 1880. Signed G. W. Schofield, Register, Jas. Gilfillan, Treasurer. The slightest application of moisture to the Treasury number printed in blue disturbs the color.

2. *Of the denomination of* $10. Check-letter D, Series of 1880, No. B, 109016. Signed as the above, photographic note one-eighth of an inch shorter and narrower than the genuine note. The seal and X's, in the genuine of pink color, have been photographed black in the counterfeit, like the balance of the note.

3. *Of the denomination of* $20. It is pen-work, poorly executed, and easily detected. The paper is thinner than the genuine, and the work appears darker. The Treasury number can be rubbed off the counterfeit with a damp finger or sponge. The diamond figures between the letters "Certificate" on the back differ in shape and size. The words "Engraved and Printed at the Bureau Engraving and Printing" are wanting on the counterfeit. They may be added, however, on the next issue.

4. *Of the denomination of* $20. No. 675114. This photographic counterfeit is much paler than the genuine.

5. *Of the denomination of* $20. Series of 1880, B1467X and B1487415X. Jas. Gilfillan, Treas. The paper is thick, greasy and stiff. The note is one-eighth inch shorter than the genuine. No distributed fibre or parallel silk threads in the paper as in the genuine. In Gilfillan only the first "i" is dotted. On back of note "Taxes" is spelled "Tares," and the word "Engraved" is spelled "Engravod." Color of the seal is brick red; should be verging on brown.

Counterfeit U. S. Treasury Notes.

Issues 1862, 1863 *and* 1869. *Nearly all the genuine are withdrawn from circulation.*

1s. Portrait of Secretary Chase. August 1, 1862.
1s. A. Wyman, Treasurer. Series 1875. Letter D.

2s. Side view of Alexander Hamilton. August 1st, 1862.
2s. Series 1875. Letter D. Photo.
5s. Left of face, female with shield. March 10th, 1863.
5s. Portrait of Jackson, Series 1875. Letter C.
5s. Vignette of Hamilton. March 10th, 1862. Letter A.
5s. Series 1875. Letter D. No. B 8058120.
5s. Series 1875. Letters A and D. No. 3420232.
10s. Portrait of Lincoln. March 10, 1862 and 1863.
10s. March 10th, 1862. Letters B and C.
10s. March 10th, 1862. Letters A, B, C, D. New Series.
10s. 1875, C. Webster's portrait blurred. Printing irregular.
20s. Female erect, with sword and shield. March 10, 1862.
20s. March 10th, 1863. Letter A. Engraving coarse.
20s. March 10th, 1863. New series, A, B, C, D.
20s. 1875. Letters A, B, C, D.
20s. 1875. A, B, C, D. Pen and ink work.
20s. 1875. Letter B. Numbered A 385285.
50s. Side view of Alex. Hamilton. March 10th, 1863.
50s. Same vignette, Alex. Hamilton. March 10th, 1862.
50s. Portrait of Clay. March 3d, 1869.
50s. U. S. Treasurer. Series of 1874. Letter A.
50s. 1875. No. 35466. Letter D. Pen and ink work.
100s. Large spread eagle on rock. March 10th, 1862.
500s. Portrait of John Q. Adams. March 3d, 1853. Plates not yet captured.
1000s. Portrait of Robert Morris. March 10th, 1862.

Unusual Check Letters on Bank Notes.

The following is a list of banks having plates bearing check letters other than A, B, C, D:—

Nat. Bank of the Republic, Boston, Mass., No. 479.— Check letters on 5s, E, F, G, H.

Manufacturers' Nat. Bank, Amsterdam, N. Y., No. 2239.— Check letters on 5s, E, F, G, H.

Lycoming Nat. Bank, Williamsport, Pa., No. 2227.—Check Letters on 1s, E, F, G, H.

First Nat. Bank, Hoboken, N. J., No. 1444.—Check Letters on 10s, D, E, F.

First Nat. Bank, Hoboken, N. J., No. 1444.—Check Letters on 20s, B.

Merchants' Nat. Bank, New Bedford, Mass., No. 799.—Check Letters on 50s, B, C, D, E.

Canadian Counterfeits.

The Canadian banks issue notes of the following denominations: 5s, 6s, 10s, 20s, 50s, and 100s. All below $5 are being withdrawn, although there are a great many 1s, 2s and 4s still in circulation, but none of recent issue.

The Dominion notes are of the denominations $1, $2, $50, $100, $500, $1000. The $6 and $7, issued by Molson's Bank of Montreal, are being withdrawn.

DOMINION OF CANADA NOTES.—1s imitation; 4s raised from 1s.

MONTREAL.—*La Banque Jacques Cartier*, 10s from 5s. *La Banque du Peuple*, 2s raised from 1s. *Bank of British North America*, 1s on the St. John's branch; 10s on the Ottawa branch and 4s on the St. John's branch—photos. *Bank of Montreal*, 1s, 2s (photo), 5s raised from 1s; 2s on the Ottawa branch. *Consolidated Bank*, refuse all 10s on this bank, as these notes were stolen and the cashier's signature forged. *Exchange Bank of Canada*, 10s raised from 5s.

QUEBEC.—*Merchants' Bank*, 10s imitation. *Quebec Bank* 5s, 10s, 20s raised from 1s.

SHERBROOKE.—*Eastern Townships Bank*, 10s raised from 5s.

TORONTO.—*Bank of Toronto*, 5s raised from 1s. *Dominion Bank*, 1s, 4s, 5s, 10s. *Canada Bank of Commerce*, 5s, 4s raised from 5s. *Ontario Bank*, 10s, imitation plates captured.

NOVA SCOTIA.—*Merchants' Bank of Halifax*, 10s, imitation.

PRINCE EDWARD ISLAND.—*Union Bank of P. E. I.*, 1s. 2s, 5s, photo.

Failed Canadian Banks.

Bank of Western Canada.
Bank of Upper Canada.
Bank of Acadia, N. S.
Commercial and Westmoreland Banks, N. B.

Bank of Clifton.
Stadacona Bank.
Colonial Bank.
Mechanics Bank of Montreal.

Continental and Colonial Paper Money.

There are so many huudred varieties that it is impossible to give the price paid for each issue in a book like this. If you have any for sale, it is best to send them in a registered letter to me and I will give you the valuation of each by return mail, provided that ten cents in silver is enclosed in your letter to pay for the labor involved. Buying prices are 25 to 50 per cent. lower than selling prices.

The United Colonies.

Philadelphia, Dated May 10, 1775.   Fine.

1	dollar,	basket and acanthus (1)..............	
2	dollars,	hand and flail (2).....................	25 cts.
3	"	heron and eagle (3)...................	25 "
4	"	boar and spear (4)....................	25 "
5	"	hand and bush (5).....................	25 "
6	"	beaver and tree (6)...................	25 "
7	"	tempest (7)...........................	25 "
8	"	harp (8)..............................	25 "
20	"	ocean, long bill (9)..................	75 "
30	"	tomb and wreath (10)..................	25 "

Philadelphia, November 29, 1775.

1	dollar,	basket and acanthus (1)..............	25 cts.
2	dollars,	hand and flail (2)....................	25 "
3	"	heron and eagle (3)...................	25 "
4	"	boar and spear (4)....................	25 "
5	"	hand and bush (5).....................	25 "
6	"	beaver and tree (6)...................	25 "
7	"	tempest (7)...........................	25 "
8	"	harp (8)..............................	25 "

Philadelphia, February 17, 1776.

Vignette, sun dial (11) with three designs of frame for each value, marked respectively " A," " B," and " C."

1/6 dollar,	A.................................	50 cts.
"	B.................................	50 "
"	C.................................	50 "
1/3 "	A.................................	50 "
"	B.................................	50 "
"	C.................................	50 "
1/2 "	A.................................	50 "
"	B.................................	50 "
"	C.................................	50 "
2/3 "	A.................................	50 "
"	B.................................	50 "
"	C.................................	50 "
1 "	basket and acanthus (1)............	35 "
2 dollars,	hand and flail (2).................	35 "
3 "	heron and eagle (3)................	35 "
4 "	boar and spear (4).................	35 "
5 "	hand and bush (5)..................	35 "
6 "	beaver and tree (6)................	35 "
7 "	tempest (7)........................	35 "
8 "	harp (8)...........................	35 "

Connecticut.

June 1, 1773.

Fine.

2 shillings 6 pence		1 50
5 shillings		1 50
10 "		1 50
20 "		1 50
40 "		1 50

January 2, 1775.

2 shillings 6 pence		2 00
5 shillings		2 00
10 "		2 00
20 "		2 00
40 "		2 00
2 "		1 00
2 shillings 6 pence		1 00
5 shillings		1 00
40 "		1 00

October 11, 1777.

Small bills, Type border.

2 pence		1 00
3 "		1 00
4 "		1 00
5 "		1 00
7 "		1 00

Delaware.

June 1, 1759.

Type with engraved border, printed by Benj. Franklin.

1 shilling		40 cts.
18 pence		40 "
2 shillings		40 "
2 shillings 6 pence		40 "
5 shillings		40 "
10 "		40 "
15 "		40 "
20 "		40 "

May 31, 1760.

Similar, printed in red and black by Benj. Franklin.

20 shillings		50 cts.
30 "		50 "
40 "		50 "
50 "		50 "

January 1, 1776.

Type with engraved border and royal arms.

		Fine.
1 shilling		30 cts.
1 shilling 6 pence		30 "
2 shillings 6 pence		30 "
4 shillings		30 "
5 "		30 "
6 "		30 "
10 "		30 "
20 "		30 "

Georgia.

1776.

Type I. Type set with three varieties of borders to each, printed in black and red and copperplate vignettes in various colors.

¼ dollar, all type			1 50
½ " "			1 50
1 " justice, blue			1 50
1 " " " small note			1 50
1 " " orange			1 50
2 dollars, floating jugs, blue			1 50
4 " caduceus, etc., blue			1 50
4 " " " brown			1 50
4 " " " orange			1 50
7 "			2 00
10 " tree and stone			1 50
20 " rattlesnake, red			1 50

September 10, 1777.

Issued for the support of the Continental Troops.

¼ dollar, all type		2 00
½ " "		2 00
¾ " "		2 00
1 " justice, red		2 00
2 dollars, ship, red		2 00
3 " soldier, red		2 00
4 " deer, red		2 00
5 " rattlesnake, blue		2 00
6 "		2 00
7 " caduceus, blue		2 00
8 " linked chain, blue		2 00

Maryland.

1740.
Fine.

1 shilling 1 50

October 1, 1748.

1 shilling 1 50
2 shillings 6 pence 1 50
10 shillings 1 50
15   " 1 50
20   " 1 50

April 6, 1751.

1 shilling 2 00

July 14, 1756.

5 shillings 2 00
10   " 2 00
15   " 2 00
20   " 2 00

January 1, 1767.

¼ dollar .... 25 cts.
½   "   .... 25 "
¾   "   .... 25 "
⅚   "   .... 25 "
½   "   .... 25 "
⅝   "   .... 25 "
⅞   "   .... 25 "
1   "   .... 25 "
2 dollars .... 25 "
4   "   .... 25 "
6   "   .... 25 "
8   "   .... 25 "

Massachusetts.

June 1, 1779.

15 pounds 2 00

December 1, 1779.

1 shilling 2 00
1 shilling 6 pence 2 00
2 shillings 2 00
2 shillings 6 pence 2 00
3 shillings 2 00

                                                              Fine.
3 shillings 6 pence..2 00
4 shillings 2 00
4 shillings 6 pence..2 00
4 shillings 8 pence..2 00
5 shillings..2 00
5 shillings 3 pence..2 00
5 shillings 4 pence..2 00
5 shillings 6 pence..2 00

January 1, 1780.

340 pounds..2 00

February 5, 1780.

15 pounds...2 00
30 " 2 00

March 18, 1780.

Very large interest-bearing note, copper plate, printed in black and red.

200 dollars 2 90

New Hampshire.

April 1, 1737.

Arms of Great Britain ; large bill.

2 shillings 2 00
3   " 2 00
5   " 2 00
10   "   or angel 2 00
1 pound...2 00
2 pounds..2 00
3   " 2 00
5   " 2 00

April 3, 1742.

Copperplate.   Type engraved.

1 shilling...2 00
2 shillings..2 00
2 shillings 6 pence 2 00
6 shillings..2 00
20   " 2 00
40   " 2 00

April 3, 1755.

Printed from copperplate, narrow bill.

                     Fine.
6 pence, squirrel 2 00
1 shilling, rabbit 2 00
3 shillings, rooster 2 00
3 shillings 9 pence, bird.............................. 2 00
5 shillings, parrot 2 00
7 shillings 6 pence, dove 2 00

Large engraved notes.

10 shillings, fox..................................... 2 00
15 " squirrel................................... 2 00
30 " stag 2 00
3 pounds, swan 2 00

June 20, 1775.

6 shillings... 2 00

July 25, 1775.

6 pence 2 00

New Jersey.

October 20, 1758.

1 shilling 1 00
1 shilling 6 pence.................................... 1 00
3 shillings 1 00
6 " 1 00
12 " 1 00
15 " 1 00
30 " 1 00
3 pounds 1 00
6 " 1 00

April 16, 1764.

Inscription in red.

1 shilling 2 00
1 shilling 6 pence.................................... 2 00
3 shillings 2 00
6 " 2 00
12 " .... 25 cts.
15 " .... 25 "
30 " .... 25 "
3 pounds .... 25 "
6 " large red and blue....................... 25 "

New York.

September 2, 1775.

		Fine.
½ dollar		1 50
1 "		1 50
2 dollars		1 50
3 "		1 50
5 "		1 50
10 "		1 50

February 17, 1776.

Type-printed; engraved ribbon above inscribed Albany County.

⅛ dollar		2 00
½ "		2 00
¾ "		2 00

August 13, 1776.

1/16 dollar		1 00
⅓ "		1 00
¼ "		1 00
½ "		1 00
2 dollars		1 00
3 "		1 00
5 "		1 00
10 "		1 00

March 15, 1780.

20 dollars		2 00

North Carolina.

April 4, 1748.

Large engraved bill with vignette.

20 shillings		2 00
30 "		2 00
40 "		2 00
3 pounds		2 00

March 9, 1754.
Large, engraved with vignette.

		Fine.
8 pence		2 00
1 shilling		2 00
3 shillings 8 pence		2 00
4 shillings		2 00
5 " squirrel		2 00
30 "		50 cts.
40 "		50 "
3 pounds		75 "

December, 1768.
Small bills, type-printed.

2 shillings 6 pence	75 cts.
5 shillings	75 "
20 "	75 "
30 "	75 "
40 "	75 "
3 pounds	75 "
5 "	75 "

Pennsylvania.

August 10, 1637.

1 shilling	2 00
1 shilling 6 pence	2 00
2 shillings	2 00
2 shillings 6 pence	2 00
5 shillings	2 00
10 "	2 00
15 "	2 00
20 " B. Franklin, printer	1 00

August 1, 1744.

1 shilling	2 00
1 shilling 6 pence	2 00
2 shillings	1 00

March 10, 1757.
Arms of Wm. Penn. Printed by B. Franklin.

5 shillings	1 00
10 "	1 00
15 "	1 00
20 "	1 00

July 1, 1757.
Printed by B. Franklin.

	Fine.
5 shillings	75 cts.
10 "	75 "
15 "	75 "
20 "	75 "

Rhode Island.
June 29, 1775.

| 9 pence | 2 00 |
| 4 shillings | 2 00 |

November 6, 1775.

6 pence	2 00
9 "	2 00
1 shilling	2 00
2 shillings	2 00
3 "	2 00
20 "	2 00
30 "	2 00

May 22, 1777.
Inscription type set.

2 pence or 36th of a dollar	2 00
3 " or 24th of a dollar	2 00
4 " or 18th of a dollar	2 00
8 " or 9th of a dollar	2 00

July 2, 1780.
Rev. guaranteed by the United States.

1 dollar	1 00
2 dollars	1 00
3 "	75 cts.
4 "	75 "
5 "	1 00
7 "	1 00
8 "	1 00
20 "	1 00

South Carolina.
April 7, 1770.
Large engraved bill, vignette below.

| 10 pounds, justice | 2 00 |
| 20 " | 2 00 |

March 24, 1774.

                                                            Fine.

80 pounds 9 shillings, certificate.................... 2 00
100 pounds... 2 00

April 20, 1775.

50 pounds, certificate............................... 2 00

May 1, 1775.

50 pounds, certificate............................... 2 00

June 1, 1775.

Large engraved bills with vignette below in circle.

5 pounds, arrows..................................... 1 00
10   "   hand and sword............................ 1 00
20   "   clasped hands............................. 2 00
50   "   woman and tree............................ 2 00
50   "   certificate............................... 2 00
25   "   tree...................................... 75 cts
50   "   trophy, no frame.......................... 75 "
100 "   hearts in wreath, no frame................ 2 00

October 19, 1776.

Engraved bill with frame and vignette.

1 dollar, palm tree.................................. 2 00
2 dollars, grape vine................................ 75 cts.
4   "   elephant................................. 75 "
6   "   wind on ocean............................ 75 "
8   "   wind on rock............................. 75 "
10   "   trophy................................... 1 00

December 23, 1776.

Wood engraving, rough brown paper.

1 dollar, tree on rock............................... 2 00
2 dollars, rooster................................... 25 cts.
3   "   well (?)................................. 2 00
4   "   ship on fire............................. 25 "
5   "   horse.................................... 25 "
6   "   camel.................................... 25 "
8   "   ship..................................... 25 "

Vermont.

February, 1781.

1 shilling... 2 00
1 shilling 3 pence................................... 2 00

	Fine.
2 shillings 6 pence	2 00
5 shillings	2 00
10 "	2 00
20 "	2 00
40 "	2 00
3 pounds	2 00

February, 1783.

Long bill with engraved frame.

136 pounds, 15 shillings, 4 pence, certificate	2 00

Virginia.

New State arms.

1/6 dollar	1 50
1/3 "	1 50
4 dollars	1 50
5 "	1 50

July, 1776.

1 shilling 3 pence	2 00
2 shillings 6 pence	2 00
5 shillings	2 00
7 shillings 6 pence	2 00
10 shillings	2 00
12 shillings 6 pence	2 00
20 shillings	2 00
2 pounds	2 00
3 "	2 00
4 "	2 00

May 4, 1778.

Same as last, written dates.

6 dollars	2 00

May 4, 1778.

Same design, with new vignette.

1/6 dollar	2 00
1/4 "	2 00
1/3 "	2 00
2/3 "	2 00
1 "	50 cts.
3 dollars	50 "
4 "	50 "
5 "	50 "
6 "	50 "
7 "	50 "
8 "	50

CONFEDERATE NOTES.

Of all classes of Paper Money which can be procured at moderate expense, these are the most interesting, both from the multiplicity of designs, and from their being the principal relics of the greatest of civil wars. The beautifully engraved notes issued at Montgomery, at the beginning of the war, (May, 1861), with the imprint of the National Bank Note Co. of New York, are especially prized.

1861. DATE WRITTEN.

National Bank Note Co.

No.	Value.		Selling Price.
1	$1000.	Montgomery. Busts of Jackson and Calhoun...	$10 00
2	500.	Montgomery. Rural scene, cattle in brook	10 00
3	100.	" Train of cars to right at depot	5 00
4	50.	Montgomery. Three negroes in field, two hoeing	5 00
5	100.	Richmond. Train of cars left. Southern Bank Note Co. ....,....................	2 00
6	50.	Richmond. Two females on bale. Southern Bank Note Co.........................	5 00

July 25, 1861.

7	$100.	Ceres and Proserpine passing left, bust of of Washington at left	1 00
8	50.	Bust of Washington in centre	50
9	20.	Ship sailing to right, 20 at left end	50
10	20.	Female riding on deer	2 00
11	10.	Female leaning on shield, Confederate flag within ....'........	1 50
12	5.	Female leaning on figure 5, sailor at left...	3 00
13	5.	Five at left end, Manrouvier...	2 00

September 2, 1861.

14	$100.	Men loading a wagon with cotton, sailor at left	40
16	50.	Moneta seated amid treasure chests	40

No.	Value.		Selling Price.
18	50.	Train of cars to left, black and red, S. B. N. Co.	5 00
19	50.	Bust of Jefferson Davis, black and green	1 00
21	20.	Female seated behind large 20, bust of Stephens at left	25
23	20.	Bust of Alex. H. Stephens in centre, black and green	3 00
24	20.	Three females in centre, black and green	4 00
25	20.	Ship sailing right, sailor at left	40
29	20.	Female kneeling beside globe, three 20's in red, S. B. N. Co.	5 00
30	10.	Negro picking cotton, Ten, 10 and X	40
31	10.	Camp scene of Gen. Marion, sweet potato breakfast	15
32	10.	Hunter at left, child at right, Ten, X—X and 10 red	40
34	10.	Group of Indians seated, X—X and Ten in red, S. B. N. Co.	3 50
35	10.	Load of cotton bales, X—X and Ten in red, bust of Oldham at left	3 00
36	10.	Two females at left with urn	40
38	10.	Female leaning on anchor, busts, Hunter left, Memminger right	50
39	10.	Same with X—X in red	50
41	10.	Female at left leaning on shield	2 00
42	5.	Group of females, Five and 5's in red, S. B. N. Co.	3 00
43	5.	Negroes loading cotton at left corner	2 00
44	5.	Machinist seated at right, boy in oval at left	2 00
45	5.	Sailor seated beside cotton bales, bust of Memminger left	20
48	5.	Bust of Memminger in centre	50
50	5.	Similar, 5's, V and Five dollars, green	30
51	5.	Female seated on cotton bale, sailor in striped shirt at left	20
54	2.	Confederacy killing the Union, bust of Benjamin at left	2 00

1862. INTEREST NOTES, DATE WRITTEN.

55	$100.	Three negroes in field, two hoeing, bust of Calhoun at left, HUNDRED in red	20
56	100.	Train of cars left, steamship at sea	10
61	100.	Same with 100 on back in green	2 00

No.	Value.		Selling Price.

June 2, 1862.

63	$2.	Confederacy killing the Union, bust of Benjamin at left..................	30
64	2.	Same with 2 and TWO in green..........	75
65	1.	Mrs. Gov. Pickens at right, steamship at sea................................	20
66	1.	Same with 1 and ONE in green...........	75

September 2, 1862.

| 66½ | $20. | Female seated, with shield............... | 2 00 |
| 67 | 10. | Female leaning on cotton bale, bust of Hunter at right...................... | 30 |

December 2, 1862.

68	$100.	Bust of Mrs. Jeff. Davis, bust of Randolph at right, green back.............	60
69	50.	Bust of Jefferson Davis in centre, black and green...........................	50
71	20.	Capitol at Nashville, bust of Stephens at right, blue back......................	25
74	10.	Capitol at Montgomery, bust of Hunter at right, pink paper, blue back..........	15
77	5.	Capitol at Richmond, bust of Memminger at right, pink paper, blue back..........	15
81	2.	Vignette fig. 2, bust of Benjamin at right, pink paper...........................	25
83	1.	Bust of C. C. Clay in centre, pink paper...	25

April 6, 1863.

86	$100.	Bust of Mrs. Davis, bust of Randolph at right, green back......................	40
87	50.	Bust of Jefferson Davis in centre, green back................................	40
91	20.	Capitol at Nashville, bust of Stephens at right, blue back......................	15
92	10.	Capitol at Montgomery, bust of Hunter at right, blue back	15
98	5.	Capitol at Richmond, bust of Memminger at right, blue back	15
104	2.	Vignette fig. 2, bust of Benjamin at right, pink paper...........................	25
109	1.	Bust of C. C. Clay in centre, pink paper...	25
112	50 cents.	Bust of Jeff. Davis, pink paper.....,	10

No.	Value.		Selling Price.

February 17, 1864.

No.	Value.	Description	Selling Price
113	$500.	Horseman and flag at left, bust of Stonewall Jackson at right..................	50
114	100.	Bust of Mrs. Jeff. Davis, blue back........	15
116	50.	Bust of Jeff. Davis, blue back	15
117	20.	Capitol at Nashville, bust of **Stephens** at right	10
118	10.	Artillery at full speed, bust of **Hunter** at right	10
119	5.	Capitol at Richmond, bust of Memminger at right	10
120	2.	Vignette fig. 2, bust of Benjamin at right ..	25
129	1.	Bust of C. C. Clay in centre	25
136	50 cents.	Bust of Jeff. Davis	10

SET OF CONFEDERATE NOTES.

50 cents to $100.00, total $188.50..................... 40

Buying Prices,
IN LOTS.

$1, $2, $20, $50, $100 Bills ....$2.00 per 100
$5 and $10 Bills.............................$1.00 per 100

MARKET VALUE.

AT WHICH I BUY ALL CURRENT FOREIGN GOLD AND SILVER
COINS AND BANK NOTES.

☞ Foreign Bullion, Nickel or Copper Coins I do not buy.

England.
GOLD.

Five Sovereigns	24 00
One Sovereign	4 80
Half-Sovereign	2 40
Double Guinea	10 25
One Guinea	5 12
One-half	2 56
One-third	1 70

SILVER.

Crown	1 15
" Anne Dei Gratia	1 15
" 1602	1 15
One-half Crown	57
" " George II.	56
Two Shillings	46
One Shilling	23
Six Pence	11
Four Pence	07
Three Pence	05
Two Pence	04
One-and-a-half Pence	03
Bank Token, 1s. 6d.	24

Bank Token, 10d. Irish	10
" 5d. "	05
Union Token, 6d. "	06

BANK NOTES.

£1	4 80
£5	24 00
£10	48 00
£20	96 00
£50	240 00
£100	480 00

British Colonies.

GOLD.

One Mohur, India	7 10
One Mohur, East India	7 08
One-half Sovereign	2 41
Newfoundland $2	1 96

SILVER.

Sierra Leone Company Dollar	80
One Dollar, 1791	80
Three Guilders	75
One Rupee	35
One-half Rupee	17
Canada 50 cents	48
" 25 "	24
" 20 "	19
" 10 "	09
" 5 "	04

Brazil and Portugal.
GOLD.

Crown	5 75
Moidore	4 75

SILVER.

960 Reis	80
300 "	25
Cruzado	45
160 Reis	22
80 "	11
40 "	05
640 "	60
500 "	20
Milreis	40

Spain.
GOLD.

Doubloon	15 50
Half Doubloon	7 70

Four Piasters	3	80
Pistole	3	80
One-half Pistole	1	90
One-quarter Pistole		90
25 Pesetas	4	75

SILVER.

Spanish Dollar		80
Old Spanish Dollar		80
Five Pesetas		85
Twenty Reals		80
Ten Reals		23
Pistareen		15
Half-Pistareen		07

France.

GOLD.

Louis d'Or	4	50
Five Francs		95
Ten "	1	90
Twenty "	3	80
Forty "	7	60
Fifty "	9	50
One Hundred Francs	19	10

SILVER.

Crown of Louis XIV.	1	00
One-quarter Crown		20
One-eighth Crown		10
Five Francs		90
Two Francs		34
One Franc		17
One-half Franc, 50 Centimes		08
Twenty Centimes		03

BANK NOTES.

	Francs	
5	Francs	90
20	"	3 80
50	"	9 50
100	"	19 00
500	"	95 00
1000	"	190 00

Austria.

GOLD.

Quadruple Ducat	8 80
One Ducat	2 20
Sovereign	6 75
One-half Sovereign	3 38
Four Florins (10 Francs)	1 90

SILVER.

Specie Dollars	80
One Florin	35

BANK NOTES.

	Guilder	
1	Guilder	38
5	"	1 90
10	"	3 80
50	"	19 00
100	"	38 00
1000	"	380 00

Mexico.
GOLD.
Doubloon	15 50
One-half Doubloon	7 75
One-quarter "	3 90
One-eighth "	1 90
One-sixteenth "	95
Twenty Pesos	19 00
Ten "	9 50
Five "	4 80
Two and a half Pesos	2 40

SILVER.
One Peso	83
Mexican Dollar	83
Maximilian Dollar	83
Eight Reals	80
One-half, Mexican	40
One-quarter, "	18
One-tenth	04
Real	08
One-half	05

Central and South America.
GOLD.
Doubloon	15 50
Half-Doubloon	7 75
Pistole	3 90
Half-Pistole	1 95
One-quarter Pistole	90
Four Escudos	7 40

SILVER.
Eight Reals	75
Four "	35

Two Reals 17
One   "   09

Chili.
GOLD.
Doubloon 15 25
Pistole 3 80

SILVER.
Chilian Dollar..................................... 76
Eight Reals.. 76
Two   "   20
One   "   10
One-half 05

Peru.
GOLD.
Doubloon 15 25
Pistole 3 80
Twenty Soles...................................... 18 50

SILVER.

One Sole	76
One-half Sole	38
One-quarter Sole	19
One-tenth	08

Germany.

GOLD.

Twenty Marks	4 70
Ten "	2 35
Five "	1 15
Ten Thalers	7 60
Five. "	3 80
Two and one-half	1 90
Fred d'Or	3 80
Double Fred D'Or	7 60
Caroline	4 70
Ducat	2 20
Five Guilders	1 90
Quintuple Ducat	11 00

SILVER.

Five Marks	1 10
Two "	44
Cne "	22
50 Pfennig, one-half Mark	11
20 "	04
Thaler	67
Double Thaler, called	1 05
Specie Dollar	80
Rix "	80
Double Guilder, called	60
One Florin	30
Half Crown	80

BANK NOTES.

5 Marks	1	15
20 "	4	70
50 "	11	75
100 "	23	50
500 "	117	50
1000 "	234	00

Italy.

GOLD.

One hundred Lire	19	00
Fifty "	9	50
Forty "	7	60
Twenty "	3	80
Ten "	1	90
Five "		90
Two Doppia	6	00
96 Livres	15	00
Sequin	2	20

SILVER.

Five Lire	90
Two "	32
One "	16
One-half Lire	07
Ten Soldi	07
Five "	03
Twenty Grani	15
Testoon	25
Scudo	85
Half Scudo	40
Crown	85

Five Paul	40
Ten "	85
Silver Lion	85
Florin	25

Switzerland.

SILVER.

Five Francs	90
Two "	34
Crown	80
Half Crown	40
Quarter Crown	20
Half Florin	18

Holland.

GOLD.

Ten Guilders	3 80
Five "	1 90

SILVER.

Three Guilders	1 10
Two-and-one-half Guilders	85
One Guilder	32
Rix Dollar	85

BANK NOTES.

10 Guilders	3 80
25 "	9 60
40 "	15 25
60 "	23 00
100 "	39 00
200 "	78 00
300 "	118 00
1000 "	390 00

Norway, Sweden and Denmark.

GOLD.

Twenty Kronors	5 20
Ten Kronors	2 60
Ducat	2 20

SILVER.

Specie Dollar, called in	80
One Rigsdaler	40
One Kronor	24
One-half Kronor	12

BANK NOTES.

1 Kronor		24
5 "		1 20
10 "		2 40
50 "		13 00
100 "		25 00
500 "		125 50
1000 "		250 00

Russia and Poland.

GOLD.

Six Rubles, Platina	4 00
Five Rubles, Platina	3 90

SILVER.

One Ruble	60
One and a half Ruble	90
One-half Ruble	30
Five Zlot	50
Three Zlot	30

BANK NOTES.

1 Ruble		47
3 "		1 40
5 "		2 35
10 "		4 70
25 "		11 75
100 "		47 00

Greece.
GOLD.
Twenty Drachms.................................. 3 50
SILVER.
Five Drachms..................................... 90

Turkey.
GOLD.
Ten Piasters..................................... 40
SILVER.
Twenty Piasters.................................. 80
Two   "   08
One   "   05

Belgium.

Gold and Silver the same as France.

Indian States.

GOLD.

Mohur... 7 10

SILVER.

One Rupee... 36
One-half Rupee...................................... 18
Quarter Rupee....................................... 08
Quarter Pagoda...................................... 30

Japan.

GOLD.

One Yen... 90
Two Yen.. 1 80

Five Yen.. 4 70
Twenty Yen...19 00

SILVER.

Itzbu 30
Five Sen... 04
Ten Sen.. 09
Twenty Sen.. 18
Fifty Sen... 40
One Yen... 80

Bank Notes.

Canada Currency................................... 99
Nova Scotia....................................... 95
Prince Edward Island Currency..................... 95
Havana Pesos Currency............................. 30
Brazilian Milreis................................... 31

RARE FOREIGN COINS.

To give a complete list of all foreign coins would require a book of several thousand pages, which would be of little value to American collectors, as there is little demand here for such coins. The prices here given are for fine specimens.

Great Britain.

The early coins in use in this country were principally Roman; from about the year 400 to 600 A.D., a series of small coins like pennies were made, called stycæ (of mixed metal) and sceattæ (of silver). These were succeeded, about the year 600, by silver pennies of Ethelbert, Cuthred, Baldred, Eadwald, Offa, Coenwlf, Berthulf, Burgred, Ciowlf, Beonna, Edmund, and other Saxon kings, followed by the sole monarchs of England, commencing with Egbert in 800, and continuing until the Norman conquest by William the Conqueror in 1066. From this time the coinage of silver pennies continued until the reign of Edward III., in 1327, when the coinage of gold, and of the larger silver pieces, commenced. Buying prices are 25 to 50 per cent. lower than selling prices.

		Fine.
Sceattæ, 400 to 600 A.D.		3 00
1 penny, Offa, 757		5 00
1 " Coenwlf, 796		5 00
1 " Berthulf, 839		5 00
1 " Bvrgred, 852		5 00
Stycæ, Headulf, 794		5 00
" Ethelred, 840		3 00
1 penny, Egbert, 800		5 00
1 " Ethelwulf, 837		5 00
1 " Ethelbert, 856		5 00
1 " Alfred the Great, 871		5 00
1 " Edward, 901		5 00
1 " Athelstan, 925		3 00
1 " Edmund, 941		4 00
1 " Eadred, 946		4 00
1 " Eadwig, 955		4 00
1 " Eadgar, 958		3 00
1 " Edward "the Martyr," 975		4 00
1 " Ethelred, 978		1 75
1 " Edmund, "Ironside," 1016		1 75

			Fine.
1 penny,	Canute "the Dane," 1017		5 00
1 "	Harold I., 1035		5 00
1 "	Hardicanute, 1040		5 00
1 "	Edward "the Confessor," 1042		2 00
1 "	Harold II., 1066		5 00
1 "	William the Conqueror, 1066, Pax Type		2 50
	(Other types from 5 to 20 dollars each.)		
1 penny,	William Rufus, 1087		7 50
1 "	Henry I., 1100		7 50
1 "	Stephen, 1135		5 00
1 "	Henry II., 1154		2 00
1 "	Richard I., 1189, French coins only		2 00
1 "	John, 1199, Irish coins only		1 25
1 "	Henry III., 1216		65
¼ "	1277-1307, Edward I		5 00
½ "	" " "		1 50
1 "	" " "		50
1 "	1307-27, Edward II		50
¼ "	1327-77, Edward III		1 50
½ "	" "		1 50
1 "	" "		75
½ groat,	" "		1 00
1 "	" "		75
¼ penny,	1377-99, Richard II		2 00
½ "	" "		2 00
1 "	" "		1 50
½ groat,	" "		3 00
1 "	" "		3 00
¼ penny,	1399-1413, Henry IV		2 00
½ "	" "		1 00
½ groat,	" "		1 00
1 "	" "		1 00
¼ penny,	1413-61, Henry V. and VI		2 00
½ "	" " "		2 00
1 "	" " "		1 00
½ groat,	" " "		1 00
1 "	" " "		1 00

½ penny, 1461-83, Edward IV 1 00

	Fine.
1 penny, 1461–83, Edward IV	3 00
½ groat, " "	1 00
1 " " "	75
½ penny, 1483–85, Richard III	4 00
1 " " "	3 00
½ groat, " "	4 00
1 " " "	3 00
½ penny, 1485–1509, Henry VII	1 00
1 " " "	1 00
½ groat, " "	1 00
1 " " "	1 00

The above four coins come in three styles: first with an open crown on the head, second with an arched crown, and third with profile to right.

1 shilling, profile to right	5 00

Henry VIII.

			Fine.
¼ penny, 1509–47, portcullis	1 00
½ " " full face	1 00
1 " " king seated	1 00
½ groat, " head of Henry VII	1 25
1 " " " "	1 00

During the reign of Henry VIII., or "Bluebeard," the coinage was greatly alloyed, both of gold and silver, so that on the silver coins with the full face, the copper showing through, he was familiarly called "Old Copper Nose."

1 penny, 1509–47, full face	2 00
½ groat, " "	1 00
1 " " "	1 00
1 shilling, " "	5 00

Edward VI.

1 penny, 1547–51, head to left	5 00
½ groat, " "	5 00
1 " " "	5 00
1 shilling, " "	1 00
¼ penny, 1551–53, portcullis	3 00
½ " " rose	3 00
3 pence, " full face	2 00
6 " " "	1 50
1 shilling, " "	1 50
½ crown, " king on horseback	7 50
1 " " "	15 00
1 penny, " king seated	3 00
1 " " rose	3 00

                                                              Fine
1 penny, 1554-58, rose, Mary	3 00
1 " " "	3 00
½ groat, " "	3 00
1 " " "	1 25
½ " 1553-58, Philip and Mary	3 00
1 " " "	2 00
6 pence, " "	2 00
1 shilling, " "	2 00

Elizabeth.

During the reign of Elizabeth the coinage from the ½ penny to the shilling, which in previous reigns, especially that of Henry VIII., had been very much debased, was restored to good silver, and the introduction of the mill and the screw in their manufacture, instead of the old process of hammer and punch, gave the coins a more even appearance, and ultimately did away with the necessity of mint-marks, with which to prove the quality of the coins from the different mints.

½ penny, 1558-1602, portcullis	2 00
3 farthings, "	3 00
1 penny, "	50
2 pence, "	50
4 " "	75
6 " "	2 00
1 shilling, "	50
1 crown, "	15 00
3 farthings, 1561-1602, dated, with rose	1 00
1 penny, "	50
2 pence, "	50
3 " "	50
4 " "	50
6 " "	50
1 shilling, "	1 25

James I.

During the reign the coins had a different mint-mark each year.

½ penny, 1603-25, portcullis	2 00
6 pence, " king's bust, dated	75
1 shilling, " "	75
½ crown, " king on horseback	4 00
1 " " "	10 00
½ penny, " rose, no inscription	1 00
1 " " " Mag. Brit.	1 00
6 pence, " king on horseback, Mag. Brit.	1 00
1 shilling, " " "	1 00

Charles I.

During the civil wars of this unhappy monarch, the mint was at one time removed to Oxford, where the college plate was turned into money, some of the larger pieces having a view of the city in the background with "Defender of the Protestant Religion," etc., on the reverse, and as the king's resources became straitened, rude pieces were coined at Pontrefact, Newark and other towns. They were of different shapes, one of the crowns having simply a V on one side and C R crowned on the other.

	Fine.
½ penny, 1625-49, rose	2 00
1 " " "	50
½ crown, " king on horse EBOR	2 00
1 " " "	5 00
1 shilling, view of city, king on horse	2 00
½ crown, " Relig. Prot., king on horse	3 00
1 " " " "	10 00
1 " " OXON " "	5 00
10 shillings, " " "	5 00
20 " " " "	5 00
1 penny, 1625-49, head of king	75
2 pence, " "	1 00
3 " " "	75
4 " " "	1 00
6 " " "	1 00
1 shilling, " "	75
½ crown, " "	3 00
1 " " "	7 50

The Commonwealth.

½ penny, 1648-60	1 00
1 " "	1 00
2 " "	75
6 " "	1 25
1 shilling, "	1 50
½ crown, "	5 00
1 " 1649-56	15 00
6 pence, 1658, head of Cromwell	5 00
1 shilling, " "	7 50
½ crown, " "	15 00
1 " " "	20 00

Charles II.

1 penny, 1660-62, profile to left	75
2 pence, " "	50

		Fine.
3 pence, 1660-62, profile to left		50
4 " " "		75
6 " " "		75
1 shilling, " "		75
½ crown, " "		5 00
1 penny, 1677-84, head to right		50
2 pence, " "		20
3 " " "		20
4 " " "		20
6 " 1662-84, "		50
1 shilling, " "		75
½ crown, " "		1 00
1 " " "		3 00

James II.

1 penny, 1685-88		75
2 " "		50
3 " "		50
4 " "		50
6 " "		75
1 shilling, "		75
½ crown, "		2 50
1 " "		3 50

William and Mary.

1 penny, 1689-94		75
2 pence, "		50
3 " "		50
4 " "		50
6 " 1693-4		75
1 shilling, 1692-3		75
½ crown, 1689-93		1 00
1 " 1691-2		3 50

About this time, owing to the scarcity of gold, a law was passed that none should be used for ornaments during the war; and in the reign of Charles II., that none be used for gilding carriages.

William III.

1 penny, 1695-1701		75
2 pence, "		50
3 " "		50
4 " "		50
6 " "		30
1 shilling, "		75
½ crown, "		1 50
1 " "		2 50

Anne.

		Fine.
1 penny,	1702-16	75
2 pence,	"	40
3 "	"	30
4 "	"	30
6 "	1703-11	25
1 shilling,	1702-11	50
½ crown	"	1 25
1 "	"	2 50

Maunday Money.

Many of the low value coins of the later sovereigns were struck only in sets of one penny, two pence, three pence and four pence, to keep up the custom of distributing small coins among the poor on Holy or Maunday Thursday of each year, when a bag of coin was handed to each person, containing a coin for each year of the king's age.

Most collectors prefer to purchase these in sets.

Charles I., set of 4 pieces, 1-2-3-4 pence	3 00
Charles II., " " "	2 00
James II., " " "	2 00
William & Mary, " " "	2 00
William III., " " "	2 00
Anne, " " "	1 75
George I., " " "	2 00
George II., " " "	1 25
George III., " " "	1 25
George IV., " " "	2 00
William IV., " " "	1 50
Victoria, " " "	60

Ireland.

Ivars I., 870-872, penny, full face	2 00
Sithric III., 989-1029, ordinary type	2 00
" " Crux "	3 50
Ivars II., 993-994	7 00
Donald, 936-980, "DYMROEX MNEGHI"	5 00
Ethelred II., 978-1016, DUBLIN penny	5 00
Cnut, 1016-1035 " . "	5 00
John, 1199-1216, "Baptist" halfpenny, Dublin	2 00
" " " " Waterford	3 00
" " Mascle farthing	5 00
" " triangle penny, Dublin	1 50
" " " " Limerick	2 00

	Fine.
John, 1199–1216, triangle penny, Waterford	5 00
" " " halfpenny, Dublin	2 50
" " " " Limerick	5 00
" " " farthing	5 00
Henry III., 1216–72, triangle penny, Dublin	2 00
Edward I. (or II.), 1272–1307, triangle penny, Dublin	1 25
" " " " " Waterford	1 50
" " " " " Cork	5 00
" " " " halfpenny, Dublin	1 50
" " " " " Waterford	2 00
" " " " " Cork	5 00
" " " " farthing, Dublin	3 50
" " " " " Waterford	3 50

Henry V., 1412–1422. The coins figured in Simon, and by him ascribed to this prince, are now known to have been issued by Henry VII.

Henry VI., 1422–61, three crown groat	5 00
" " crown penny	5 00
Edward IV., 1461–83, groat; crown—cross	5 00
" " " head—rose and sun	5 00
" " " " head, Waterford	1 75
" " " " Dublin	1 75
" " " " Trim	3 50
" " " " Drogheda	3 50
" " " " Limerick	5 00
" " " " Cork	5 00
" " " " Wexford	5 00
" " " three crowns	1 75
" " half groat, head—rose and sun	5 00
" " " head, Dublin	5 00
" " " three crowns, Dublin	2 50
Richard III., 1483–85, groat; head	5 00
" " " three crowns	7 50
Henry VII., 1485–1509, groat; three crowns	2 00
" " " head with arched crown	3 00
" " " head with flat crown	2 00
" " half groat; three crowns	5 00
Henry VIII., 1509–47, groat; shield—harp	1 50
" " " shield, with title, "REX"	1 75
" " " shield, with initials of queens,	1 50
" " sixpence; head—shield	1 00
" " " shield—harp, "37"	1 75
" " " shield—harp, "38"	1 75
Mary, 1553–54, shilling; head—harp	10 00
" " groat; head—harp	5 00
" " half groat; head—harp	5 00
" " penny; head—harp	5 00

Fine.

Philip and Mary, 1554-58, shilling; heads vis-a-vis—harp. 3 50
    "   "   "   groat;   "   "   "   1 50
Elizabeth, 1558-1602, shilling; head; of fine silver......4 00
    "   "   "   shield; of base metal....3 50
    "   "   "   head; of base metal.....3 50
    "   "   groat; head; of fine silver........10 00
    "   "   "   "   of base metal........3 50
    "   "   sixpence; shield; of base metal....2 00
    "   "   threepence; shield; of base metal..5 00
James I., 1603-25, shilling; first coinage...............1 50
    "   "   "   second coinage............1 50
    "   "   sixpence; first coinage..............1 50
    "   "   "   second coinage...........1 50
Charles I., 1625-49, Inchiquin crown...................5 00
    "   "   Ormonde   " 10 00
    "   "   Rebel   " 5 00
    "   "   Rebel half-crown...................5 00
    "   "   Ormonde half-crown.................7 50
    "   "   "   shilling 4 00
    "   "   "   sixpence 3 50
    "   "   "   groat 5 00
    "   "   "   threepence 5 00
    "   "   "   twopence...............5 00
    "   "   Cork shilling......................5 00
    "   "   "   sixpence......................5 00
Charles II., 1660-85, Dublin crown.....................5 00
    "   "   "   half-crown................5 00

Scotland.

1 penny, 1163-1214, William 2 00
1 " Alexander I., II., III...........................2 00
1 " Robert I., II., III..............................2 00
1 " 1329-71, David II..............................2 00
½ groat, " " 2 00
1 " " " 3 00
1 " 1437-60, James II............................1 50
1 penny, 1542-1587, Mary, billon....................2 00
1 groat, " " " 3 00
½ tostoon or 6d., 1553, " 3 00
1 " or 1s., " " 3 00

		Fine.
10 shillings, 1565, Mary, XX		5 00
20 " " " XXX		5 00
1 crown, " " palm tree		5 00
½ mark or 1 shilling, 1571-78, James VI		3 00
½ " 1625-49, Charles I		3 00
½ " 1660-62, Charles II		3 00

After the reign of Queen Anne the coins of Scotland were merged with the United Kingdom.

France.

The earliest coins of France were made in the time of the Emperor Clovis, followed by rude coins of Pepin and Charlemagne, the gold coinage of Philip of Valois, the base silver of St. Louis, the gold crowns of Chas. VII., and the silver gros or groats of Louis XII. and Henry II., succeeded by the regular coinage of crowns and half-crowns in the reign of Louis XII.

1 penny, Charlemagne, 814				5 00
½ groat, Charles VII., fleur de lis				75
1 " Louis XII., "				1 00
1 " Henry II., "				1 00
5 sols, 1640-1713, Louis XIV				50
10 " " "				35
20 " " "				50
¼ crown, " "				1 00
½ " " "				2 00
1 " " "				3 50
10 sols, 1721-31, Louis XV., to right				50
20 " " " "				50
¼ crown, " " "				1 25
½ " " " "				2 00
1 " " " "				3 50
10 sols, 1726-35, " bust to left				50
20 " " " "				50
¼ crown, " " "				1 25
½ " " " "				2 00
1 " " " "				2 00

                                                                  Fine.
10 sols, 1745-73, Louis IV., head to left.................. 50
20 "   "   "   "   50
¼ crown,   "   "   " 1 25
½ "   "   "   "   " 1 50
1 "   "   "   "   " 1 50
10 sols, 1777-92, Louis XVI., bust to left.................. 50
20 "   "   "   "   50
¼ crown,   "   "   " 1 25
½ "   "   "   " 1 00
1 "   "   "   " 1 75
15 sols, 1791-3.. 50
30 "   "   75
½ crown,   " 1 00
1 "   " 2 00
6 livres, 1793.. 2 00
5 francs, anno 7-11, like 1848........................... 1 75
¼ franc, 11-12, Napoleon I., Consul..................... 1 00
5 francs anno 11-12, Napoleon I., Consul................ 2 00
¼ franc, "   12-13, "   Emperor............... 40
½ "   "   "   "   " 1 00
1 "   "   "   "   "   50
5 francs, "   "   "   " 2 00
5 "   1806   "   " 2 00
¼ franc, 1808, laureated, rev. Republic................. 50
½ "   "   "   "   "   50
1 "   "   "   "   "   40
5 francs, 1806-8,   "   " 2 50
¼ franc, 1809-13, laureated, rev. Empire................ 50
½ "   "   "   "   "   50
1 "   "   "   "   "   50
2 francs, "   "   "   " 1 00
5 "   "   "   "   " 2 00
5 "   1815, 100 days................................ 3 50

Spain.

2 reales, 1567-92, Philip II............................. 1 00
4 "   "   " 1 50
8 "   "   " 3 00
1 real,   1632, Philip IV............................... 1 00
8 reales,   "   " 3 00
1 real,   1675, Charles I............................... 75
1 "   1686-95, Charles II........................... 50

Rude coins with pillars and cross.

¼ real, 1611-1721...................................... 20
½ "   "   30
2 reales "   30

During the reign of Philip II., king of Spain, coins were made of rude pieces of metal, for use in America, with shield or pillars on one side, and a cross on the other, which divides it into sections resembling the broken end of a corn cob.

		Fine.
½ real, 1712–63, cob money		20
1 " " "		30
2 reales, " "		30
4 " " "		50
8 " " "		2 00

The above were often clipped and went largely by weight in connection with dollars cut into small pieces.

½ real, 1709–81, Charles III	15
1 " " "	20
2 reales, " "	40
4 " " "	50
1 pistareen, 1709–81, Charles III	25
8 reales, or dollar, 1709–81, Charles III	2 00
¼ real, 1717–42, Philip V	10
½ " " "	10
1 " " "	15
2 reales, " "	25
4 " " "	75
8 " or dollar, 1717–42, Philip V	2 00
2 " 1724, Louis I	3 00

Old German Crowns.

In making a collection of foreign silver coins many collectors prefer to make as complete a series as possible of dollar or crown size. Of these one of the most interesting are the old medallic crowns of the cities and princes of Germany and Holland from the 15th to the 17th century. We always have a large variety of these in stock, and describe some of the most interesting, though a complete collection would number several hundred. There were also a few half crowns issued, as well as double, triple and quadruple crowns. For a complete description of these crowns see the *Coin Collector's Journal* for 1875. Buying prices are 25 to 50 per cent. lower than selling prices.

	Fine.
John George of Saxony, 1628-55	3 00
" " 1657, Deo et Patriæ	4 00
" " 1586, a whole book on the coin	4 00
" " 1656, king in circle	5 00
" " 1530, Lutheran Confession	6 00
Frederick, 1643, German legend	3 00
Frederick Augustus, 1711, on horse, funereal	4 00
Frederick Albert and brothers, 1629, Brand	3 00
Three brothers of Saxony, 1624-29	3 00
Eight brothers of Saxony, 1610, four heads on each side	5 00
George, Duke of Saxony, 1530, Altenburg	4 00
Frederick William, 1579, reverse John of Saxony	4 00
John Frederick and Henry of Saxony, 1540	3 00
Sigismund, duke of Austria, 1486, dated	15 00
" Episcopate of Salisbury, 1760	5 00
Paris, archbishop of Salisbury, 1650	4 00
John, " " 1571	5 00
Julius of Brunswick, wild man	3 00
Henry Julius. 1596, angel crowning lion	6 00
Wild man and dog, 1595, rev. seven shields	6 00
Ernest Augustus, 1667, wild man standing	4 00
Wild man of Hartz mountains, 1658-79	4 00
Sigismund III., king of Poland, 1628	4 00
John Casimir and John Ernest, 1585	4 00
" " " 1625, heads each side	4 00
Martin Luther, 1661, (base silver)	3 00
William, landgrave of Hesse, 1637, lion	5 00
½ Bell, Thaler, Bust R Bell, 1643	5 00
Bruns. and Luneburg, Augustus, bell, 1643	4 00
" " " clapper, 1643	4 00
" " 1630, Christian, large head	3 00
" " Charles, 1752, swan in harbor	5 00
Ratisbon, Francis, 1754, Thaler, view of city	3 50
Mansfield, 1609, St. George and Dragon	4 00
" 1671, " order of the Garter	6 00

	Fine.
Henneburg, 1696, large hen	4 00
" 1699, farcical scene	4 00
Henry Julius, wasp thaler, 1597	5 00
Ferdinand II., 1626, standing figure	3 00
" large head	3 00
Ferdinand III., 1655, very large head	3 00
" 1639, view of city of Augsburg	3 00
" 1658, Bohemia	4 00
Westphalia, view of the monastery, 1661	5 00
Thuringia, three brothers	4 00
Belgium, 1759, horseman, rev. lions	4 00
Ragusa, 1777, bishop in robes	3 00
Schaffhausen, 1622, goat and eagle	3 00
Burgundy, Equestrian, 1603, Admiral	4 00
" Leopold with mitre, 1630	3 00
" and Tyrol, 1626, Leopold	3 00
Leopold, Tyrol, 1692, "hogmouth"	3 00
Frederick, king of Sweden, 1720, "Hope in God"	3 00
Louis I., prince of Siliste, very old	3 00
Denmark, 1659, sword cutting off hand	4 00
" Christian IV., 1648, lion	4 00
Rudolph, 1603, Hungary and Bohemia	3 00
Rudolph II., 1589, Austria	3 50
Anna Sophia, 1675, ⅔ crown, Quedlinburg	5 00
George Albert, 1538-44, two heads facing	3 00
Sigismund Bathori, 1592, Transylvania	4 00
Hamburg, 1553, gate with towers	5 00
Luneberg, 1547, man in the moon	4 00
Lubeck, 1752, double eagle	3 00

Double Crowns.

Ferdinand Charles, Archduke of Austria	6 00
Leopold, Archduke of Austria	8 00
Leopold and Claudia, of Austria	8 00
Ferdinand II., and Eleonora, 1622	8 00
Rudolph Augustus, 1679, horseman	15 00
Brunswick coronation, 1½ crown, 1666	10 00
John Casimir, duke of Saxony, 1625, horseman	10 00

Triple Crowns.

Ernest Augustus, of Brunswick, 1664, horse jumping over Hartz mountain silver mines	25 00
Augustus on horseback, Brunswick and Luneberg, 1662	15 00
John George of Saxony, 1622, horseman	25 00
" " 1650, king standing	15 00

A Few Explanations

ABOUT GREEK AND ROMAN COINS.

No doubt it seems strange to the superficial observer that coins issued 1500 to 2500 years ago should not bring as much as some coined a few years ago, but this is a fact, and genuine Greek and Roman copper coins the size of a dime do seldom bring over 25 cents apiece; those of the size of a quarter to half dollar, 50 to 75 cents; and those of the size of a silver dollar, $1.00 to $5.00. Of course these prices apply to common varieties. Rare issues bring some very high prices. There are such large quantities of these old coins constantly unearthed, that the supply far exceeds the demand. These coins are old but not rare. Now, anyone not familiar with these old coins will say: "How do you know that they are so old; there is no date on them?" Coins never were dated as they are now until about 1450 A.D. The only way to determine the age of Greek and Roman coins is to look up ancient history. Most of the ancient coins, as far back as 300 years before Christ, have on the obverse, like those of the present day, the bust of some prince, king, tyrant or emperor; and on the reverse, the title or name. Now, if one is familiar with the Greek or Latin language, it is very easy to find out under whose reign the coin was issued, and by consulting the chronology one can ascertain the age of a coin within a very narrow limit. On the following plates are given some illustrations of these early coins: Those on the first plate were coined 700 to 600 B.C., those on the second 300 to 200 B.C., those on the third from 60 to 100 A.D., and those on the fourth plate from 1000 to 1670 A.D.

To a student of ancient history nothing can be more interesting than these coins, as some are relics and witnesses of the former existence of cities and nations, which if it were not for these coins we never should have known anything of their existence.

SILVER COINS OF THE EARLIEST PERIOD.

GREEK COINS OF PRINCES.

COINS OF THE FIRST XII CÆSARS, &c., &c.

COINS OF THE ENGLISH SERIES.

FIRST ENGLISH SHILLING (HENRY VII)
GOLD NOBLE OF EDWARD III
SIXPENCE OF THE COMMONWEALTH
SILVER PENNY OF WILLIAM I
SILVER PENNY OF EDWARD I
SILVER PENNY OF ÆTHELSTAN
SILVER CROWN OF CHARLES II
(THE FAMOUS PETITION CROWN)

GOLD COINS OF THE EARLIEST PERIOD.

GREEK COINS OF THE FIRST PERIOD.

ATHENS

DELPHI

GELAS

EPHESUS

SYRACUSE

H121.74

www.ingramcontent.com/pod-product-compliance
Lightning Source LLC
Chambersburg PA
CBHW032229230426
43666CB00033B/1652